900
ark
1/17

# The Challengers

# *The Challengers*

Untold Stories of African Americans Who Changed the System in One Small Southern Municipality

The NAACP Hot Springs Unit 6013
Presents profiles of 63 black candidates who filed for political office in Hot Springs, Arkansas, from 1954–2010

## Elmer Beard

Library of Congress Cataloging-in-Publication Data
Beard, Elmer

The Challengers / by Elmer Beard

Cover and Interior Design by Lon Edward Ware II
Editors: John Archibald, Katherine Wright Knight, and Sonya Beard

**ISBN 9780692606988**
Hot Springs Arkansas History, 1954–2010. 2. Arkansas History, 1954–2010. 3. African American. 4. American Biography.
**Library of Congress Control Number 2015921111_**
Published in the United States of America

Freedom's Price Publishing
P. O. Box 1105
Hot Springs National Park, Arkansas
71902

# Dedication

This book is dedicated to the memory
of my late wives

**Dorothy Mae Beard**

and

**Wilhemina Franklin Beard**

The cover design is a tribute to the
blue and gold school colors
of the historic Langston High School

# Table of Contents

(D) indicates the candidate is deceased

X

# Acknowledgements

First, I would like to thank my Lord and Savior Jesus Christ for allowing me to live long enough to see this project become a reality.

As the author, I wish to thank the NAACP Unit 6013 for its cooperation and support. Indebtedness also is due the NAACP Writing Project Committee: Linda Franklin, Fred Leonard, Bob Freeman, Lavenia Hicks, Diane White, Tim Pentecost, and Precious Williams.

I also want to thank my typist, Ann Works, for her invaluable assistance. A special thanks is in order to my editor John Archibald for his tireless work. English teacher Katherine Wright Knight was also a tremendous help. My daughter Sonya Beard, a professional journalist, and the graphic-designing guru Lon Ware were instrumental in finally getting the book into publication. The legal expertise from Attorney John Howard was invaluable.

I am grateful to the administrative staff at the Garland County Clerk's Office for digging through decades-old public records to complete these profiles. John Wells, at the Garland County Library, was also a great resource.

Lastly, I want to thank the several people who opened their scrapbooks, photo albums, and keepsake drawers to share memories, photos, obituaries, and political papers.

This book was made possible in part by the generous financial contributions from Kenneth Rhodes, the Oaklawn Scholarship Foundation, the Arkansas Humanities Council, the Arkansas Black History Commission, and the Clinton Family Foundation.

Lift Every Voice and Vote!
*Black Leadership Forum, 1998*

# Introduction

From the late 19th Century through World War II, nearly all of the public officials in the City of Hot Springs had been white. There are reports of two black men—Jackson D. Page and J.H. Golden—elected to the city council on April 5, 1886, according to *The Record*, a yearbook from the Garland County Historical Society.

Another exception, though scarcely documented, was a black man named J.H. Carr. Little is known about Carr and his tenure as a police judge in the late 1890s or the early 1900s. Some even questioned if Carr was so fair-skinned that he passed for white, as Alderman Theodore Page was quoted in an early 1960s edition of the local black newspaper, *The Arkansas Citizen*. Any official records of Carr's candidacy went up in flames during the Garland County Court House fire in 1905.

In the African American oral tradition, however, there was always word-of-mouth to preserve black history. *The Challengers: Untold Stories of How African Americans Changed the System in One Small Southern Municipality* is a modern attempt to etch that history into public record.

This story begins in 1954. The U.S. Supreme Court in a ground-breaking decision, *Brown v. Board of Education of Topeka, Kansas,* reversed its national law of separate-but-equal public accommodations from its earlier 1896 decision, *Plessy v. Ferguson.* The *Brown* decision was a powerful breakthrough in the human rights struggle for equality, particularly for black Americans.

In 1954, the Spa City experienced a political breakthrough of its own. That November, Fred W. Martin, a black man, ran for office. In previous elections, a white man named Clifford Martin had repeatedly run and won. This time the setting was different. The black voters knew who they wanted to win the election. By contrast, hundreds of white voters unknowingly thought they were voting for the white Martin instead of the black Martin. White voters unintentionally voted for the son of a former slave on Election Day, November 2, 1954.

"Negro Leads Council Race" reported a top story of *The Sentinel-Record* newspaper on Wednesday, November 3, 1954. "A Negro citizen was well on his way to becoming the first member of his race elected to the city council, on the face of incomplete and unofficial returns from yesterday's general election," the story reported.

In a conversation during the 1960s, Fred W. Martin explained how chaos erupted at the Garland County Court House after the tally had been counted, and this news report appeared the morning after Election Day. A mob of white residents crammed into the courthouse and the clerk's office, as seen by a janitor who later told Martin about it. The citizens demanded that they be able to change their vote. The county clerk declined their request, Martin said.

Fred Martin took the oath of office in January 1955. The NAACP Writing Project Committee referred to the matter as the **"Martin Mix-Up"** of the mid-20th Century.

Fred Martin served his two-year term. He ran for re-election and lost, according to November 1956 records in the county courthouse. In that election, white voters knew which candidate was the black Martin. Undaunted, Martin ran for office two more times after 1956. He lost both times, in 1957 and again in 1960. Martin won just once out of four attempts. White voters knew his name in the second, third, and fourth times. They had learned their lessons the hard way and would not make the same mistake again. The experiment was pretty remarkable in gauging the political climate during that era.

Despite the history of previous black elected officials in Hot Springs and Garland County, there was only a dim memory of them by 1954. That is why Fred W. Martin was mistakenly reported as "the first member of his race elected to the city council." The system had forgotten about the earlier black elected officials, which is indicative of much of the history in the black community. This is why this book looks at history from 1954–2010 through the eyes of the 63 black candidates who experienced it. Many of the stories are encapsulated here for the first time.

Through countless court documents, funeral programs, newspaper articles, and interviews from relatives, friends, and many of the candidates themselves, we have gathered information about the political climate in which these *Challengers* filed, ran, lost, and won.

Now the challenge is issued to other NAACP chapters, civic organizations, or church groups throughout Arkansas and the rest of the country to do the same: Go beyond carrying on the oral tradition by documenting the black political involvement in your municipality.

# Kenneth Adair

In 1985, Alderman Kenneth Adair, a civil rights activist and journalist, was serving his seventh two-year term on the Hot Springs City Council when the mayor-alderman **form of government** was coming to a storied end. He had been a staunch supporter of the city council system, which was being replaced by a city manager and board of directors. During his terms on the council, he became one of the most outspoken officials the city has ever known.

Adair suggested the city council approve the hiring of a female supervisor to attend to the personal care of the female prisoners; it was the first time a position was designated for a jail matron in the city's history. A free blood-pressure service was established in his ward; the health screenings were available to all residents citywide. Even at his very first council meeting, Adair and Alderman Elmer

Kenneth Adair

Beard cast the only two dissenting votes against a resolution to reinstate the death penalty.

Adair forged many partnerships with Beard throughout their career. The two Ward 3 aldermen would make it their mission to seek grants for public works in their community,

**Bill Ott, Kenneth Adair, Art Merkel, Elmer Beard, and Tom Ellsworth**

which eventually would become a part of the Public Works Program for the City of Hot Springs. About $725,000 was allocated and invested in previously overlooked neighborhoods during the 1970s, said retired City Manager Lance Hudnell in an August 2014 interview. These neighborhoods were disproportionately black.

Adair served on and later became chairman of the Public Works Committee. With this chairmanship, an increase in public works funding was inevitable for Ward 3. Former Mayor Tom Ellsworth admitted that Wards 3 and 5 had been neglected prior to the 1970s. Soon paved streets with curbs and gutters became the norm for these areas. The struggles of the 1950s and 1960s bore fruit in the 1970s.

Out of those efforts came the popular neighborhood hangout Chattanooga Park, which opened in September 1977. It took years of striving and struggling for the park to become a reality for black residents in the area.

Before he became an elected official, Adair owned and published a local black newspaper, *The Arkansas Citizen.* Adair had used the newspaper, since its inception in 1958, as a platform to advance the less fortunate. He also used the press to promote the mayor-alderman form of government. According to an interview with *The Sentinel-Record* on January 15, 1985, he said, "I ran for alderman six times before it was even possible for me to be an alderman, to protest citywide elections."

Before 1970, Hot Springs aldermen could be elected by people who didn't live in the ward of the candidate. This way, voters could influence the outcome of candidates in other wards—and this kept black candidates out of politics. This method was called the election of alderman via **at-large voting** and that was the way that **the system** worked. After 1970, the political system changed to the current **one-**

**The February 1985 edition of *The Arkansas Citizen***

**man, one-vote system**. In the new system, only candidates who lived in a ward could receive votes from people who had a legal residence in that ward.

In November 1970, Adair ran as a republican against Ray Smith Jr. for a state representative position. The final vote count was Ray Smith, democrat, 13,446 votes compared to Kenneth Adair, republican, at 4,217 votes, according to the Garland County Clerk's Office. At the time of the campaign, Adair was serving as both an alderman for the City of Hot Springs and as president of the local branch of the **National Association for the Advancement of Colored People** (NAACP) Unit 6013.

From his boyhood days, this freedom fighter wanted to be a prize fighter. He took up boxing as a teenager, fighting to make a living. During the 1920s and into the 1930s, he fought "successfully as a way to eat. You could always go into a club during those days and get a fight," Adair said in *The Sentinel-Record*. He traveled widely during his boxing years to Kansas City, Kansas; St. Louis, Missouri; and Detroit, Michigan.

Meanwhile, Adair worked as a waiter in many hotels, trying to organize unions in most of them, which led to his termination in every case. His most dependable job had been in the dry-cleaning business. Retiring to Hot Springs, Adair worked stints as a manager of both the Pythian Hotel and a nearby tailor's shop on the famed Malvern Avenue.

During the 1980s, his newspaper had some of the oldest printing equipment used in Arkansas—it had an ancient Linotype type-setting machine. All of the copies were free during the last years of production. Though the newspaper building still stands at 515 Pleasant Street, in 2010 it had been converted into a private real estate office.

Being married to the media and politics, or at least living with both, Adair was a courageous social activist who ran for office more than a dozen times in his lifetime and was a candidate for four different positions. This was over a period of more than 25 years. An octogenarian who was warned by his wife to slow down, he worked until his health declined. He fought until the end.

In downtown Hot Springs, Adair Park is named in his honor. The businessman was loved, admired, and revered by many in the community. He was a threat of whom to be reckoned. He left an enduring impression on the have-nots during his career in politics as an alderman and leader. Baptist minister Dr. W.J. Thomas had one word to describe Kenneth Adair: "warrior."

---

## Adair's Fight for Civil Rights

The people's fighter Kenneth Adair always sided with the marginalized residents of society. With the history of racism in America, Adair declared that he was always right in the fight for civil and human rights even if he was wrong. Adair defended the downtrodden, with or without all the facts, against cases of police brutality and various other forms of injustice. Even his haters in the media respected him.

—*Elmer Beard, colleague and friend*

# Thomas J. Anderson

Thomas James Anderson has given more than a decade and a half of service to Garland County. Thomas and his sister, Vicky Anderson, are the only African American brother-sister duo who ran for public office. Their filing showed their unselfish attitude toward their community.

In 2015, Anderson was serving as District 2 Justice of the Peace on the Garland County Quorum Court. Anderson, a veteran public official serving his 16th year as he completes his eighth two-year term, reflected that he didn't seek a career in politics.

**Thomas J. Anderson**

A major concern that Anderson addressed was the lack of support from constituents in the courtroom where the Quorum Court held its meetings. Anderson and the local NAACP have searched for a cure for the apathy that has been prevalent among far too many black voters. His solution was to encourage more attendance in the courtroom.

Effective elected officials often invite residents to serve on committees, boards, and commissions. In May 2002, Anderson submitted the names of Sadie S. Stamps and Hazel M. Wright as prospective appointees to the Garland County Library Board.

Anderson won the admiration of several people over the years, including Mary Culpepper, the chief of staff to

10

Garland County Judge Rick Davis. Culpepper characterized Anderson as being conservative and added, "He's easy to work with, and he is a personal friend of mine."

There was a bit of controversy during Anderson's tenure on the Quorum Court. It is important to recall because it shows how the participation of African Americans fostered a better political climate in Hot Springs. Anderson and Aaron Gordon were vying for the same position of District 2 Justice of the Peace. Gordon filed an official grievance of residency against Anderson with the Garland County Central Democratic Committee, according to *The Sentinel-Record* on May 16, 2000.

In the complaint, Anderson's car was seen at different hours of the day and night at the home of his new wife, Mozella. She lived in a different district. Gordon raised the question, which district did Anderson intend to occupy for representation?

Anderson satisfied the Democratic Committee by clarifying he intended to keep living in his house in District 2, and his wife, Mozella, would be keeping her house. Anderson stayed in the race after a vote by the executive committee ruled that he was not in violation of the residency guidelines.

Anderson and Gordon handled their differences with class. The resolution of the dispute happened in a civil, professional way long before the election, unlike the Martin Mix-Up four decades earlier when angry voters stormed the courthouse. This time, an amicable solution was reached. Anderson eventually won the election.

Described by some as being resourceful and methodical, Anderson was a police detective sergeant for more than

20 years and has been an Arkansas probation-parole agent since 1996. He was in the ninth class of Leadership Hot Springs, an educational program to develop community leaders. Anderson graduated from the segregated Langston High School and earned an associate's degree in criminal justice from the Garland County Community College, now known as the National Park College. He serves as a trustee at Greater St. Paul Baptist Church and holds a list of other memberships in his community.

Anderson is credited with much of the success and the diversity of the Dr. Martin Luther King Jr. Prayer Breakfast, an annual event that recognizes the birthday, struggle, and legacy of the slain civil rights leader.

# Vicky Anderson

Vicky Anderson, like her brother Thomas, felt a need to serve. In 1995, Anderson made an unsuccessful bid for a position on the Hot Springs School Board, but she didn't see the election as a loss.

**Vicky Anderson**

She saw herself as a person who understood the importance of investing more time in the community. Anderson said she had vivid memories of Election Day as a child: "I was inspired by the push to vote when I was young. My mother took me with her when she voted. They asked my mother if I was registered to vote, and she told them I was too young. I've tried to instill in my adult child the value of voting."

Anderson's motivation to seek office was born out of negative interactions with educators in school and the positive encouragement from mentors throughout her career. In junior high school, Anderson remembers trying to improve her vocabulary without being instructed by a teacher. "I liked to look for the definition of new words. I'd find a way to practice the words during the day. While I was in study hall, a male teacher made a comment about how, 'Black people do not look for words in the dictionary,' and the other black students laughed," Anderson said. The teacher teased her calling her "Professor Anderson." From that day on, she stopped trying to learn new vocabulary words. Anderson, who had been enrolled in special education courses, said many teachers had low expectations of black students making above a "C" grade. They were, however, interested in passing them on to the next grade.

She vowed to encourage her daughter to form her own opinion and stressed the power of reading, Anderson said. "I invested a lot of money in books for my child. I took her to the library to check out books regularly."

After Anderson graduated from high school, she earned a bachelor of science in social work from Kansas State University and a master of science in social work from the University of Tennessee. She is also a licensed master's social worker. Anderson proudly recalled that with very limited assistance, she struggled through college and during some semesters she only took classes based on her income and ability to pay. Her social work preparation carried her to Lincoln, Nebraska, to work for one year.

Later, Anderson said it gave her great pleasure when she returned to her old high school and spoke with one of her counselors who had not encouraged her to further her education and did not provide her with information about college scholarships. When the counselor heard her story about graduating from college, "the shock" on the counselor's face was priceless, she remembered.

Dr. Van Davis inspired Anderson while she was taking classes at the Garland County Community College, now known as the National Park College. He played a major role in her self-perception. She no longer felt like just a "C" student. "I was an 'A' student," Anderson recalled Davis telling her. After she earned her degree, Anderson returned to the college to share her educational accomplishments with Davis.

Alroy Puckett was another positive role model in her life, she said. Her role model in her work was Police Lieutenant Bill Watkins. Anderson credited her family and several other people for her determined strides toward her degrees and profession. They include retired police Captain Willie McCoy and former Hot Springs School Superintendent Joyce Craft. A warden, Marvin Evans, encouraged Anderson to be more proactive while they were working at the Arkansas Department of Corrections.

However, it was Annette Butler, a school board member, who convinced her to run for an open position on the Hot Springs School Board. Although it was an unsuccessful bid, Anderson believed her campaign stood for something more, she said. "I ran for the office because I believed I could help students achieve success."

# Elmer Beard

Elmer Beard, an eight-term city councilman, is the self-appointed dean of politics in the African American community in Hot Springs. In 1969, Beard helped to establish the city's first majority-minority district and the current one-man, one-vote system. He was a long-time president of the **NAACP Unit 6013**; now he is the secretary and elder passing the baton of leadership to its younger members.

**Elmer Beard**

Beard served his community as an alderman for a total of 15 years, 5 months, 20 days, and 30 minutes. The politician filed for public office 13 times: eight elections were for alderman, four were for mayor, and one was for Justice of the Peace on the Garland County Quorum Court. He had a 14th election when he was in a run-off for justice of peace; he lost the race to Leonard Dunn.

In the 1970s, Beard recalled Virginia Clinton Kelley introducing him to her son Bill, a Yale Law School graduate. In his first political campaign, Bill Clinton would take on the popular republican incumbent U.S. Representative John Paul Hammerschmidt. Many local democrats shied away from supporting Clinton in his David-and-Goliath bid. Beard, however, supported the hometown politician, advising Clinton on how to connect with black voters. The 42nd president would lose that election in 1974, his first of only two losses on his journey to the White House.

When Beard was a first-time candidate for alderman in 1970, he ran as a Christian, an educator, and a leader. The Chidester native said he studied high men in low places and low men in high places. He knew that a position in public office belonged to the people and that he was entrusted with it for a limited amount of time.

Beard finished in first place, and fellow African American candidate Theodore Page finished in second place. Voting results were as follows: Beard, 661; Page, 501; Walker, 252; Rosborough (Sr.), 246; White, 235; Bratton, 227; and Gooden, 99, according to the Garland County Clerk's Office.

In the 1972 election, there were only three candidates, instead of seven, vying for the two positions in Ward 3. Kenneth Adair finished in first place, Beard in second, and Theodore Page in third. Adair and Beard won the election, with Beard overcoming Page by nearly 60 votes, according to the November 3, 1970, edition of *The Sentinel-Record.*

In 1973, during the first city council meeting that Beard and Adair attended together, a resolution was read asking the city to support the reinstatement of the death penalty. The votes were 10–2 in favor of the resolution, with Adair and Beard having cast the dissenting votes. Both aldermen contended that the blacker and poorer one was, the sooner one would get the electric chair. The news media gave statewide coverage to the story and the vote.

The struggle to fight inequality continues. Too often the success of African American elected officials was measured by news coverage, controversial issues, and the opposition that they created. Some of the issues that endured weren't very dramatic but had long-lasting appeal.

CONVENTION AUDITORIUM
HOT SPRINGS, ARKANSAS
JULY 14, 1969, 7:30 P.M.
BI-RACIAL COMMITTEE - C.L.O.B.

PROGRAM

Invocation ----------------------------------------------Rev. M. R. White
Welcome and Introduction of Bi-Racial Committee - Garland Puckett
The Bi-Racial Committee---------------------------Dr. George F. Ivey
Objective of C.L.O.B. and Community Problems---John Paschal, President
Remarks--------------------------------------------------Garland Puckett
Benediction---------------------------------------------Rev. M.R. White

An artifact of the civil rights past, this late 1960s agenda is for a program for the Council for the Liberation of Blacks.

One of those lasting changes was Beard's involvement in the **Council of the Liberation of Blacks** (CLOB), in a successful protest to have the city re-draw the lines of the wards. Following a resolution to the council made by CLOB members in 1969, then-Mayor Dan Wolf and the city council consulted with City Attorney Curtis Ridgway. Ridgway advised the city council to appoint a special committee to resolve the re-apportionment of the wards. Attorney Henry M. Britt, who later became a circuit judge, served as chairman of the three-member committee. Beard and both chairmen from the Democrat and Republican parties were appointed to the committee, which was named the **Garland County Re-Apportionment Commission.**

For several months, the re-apportionment commission met, studying local maps, census records, and population history. It re-drew lines until a majority district was created. The results saw a reduction in wards from eight to six. It also increased the size of each ward. Many present aldermen were then in the same ward, and no current alderman at that time lived in Ward 3, the soon-to-be legendary ward because it became a minority-majority ward.

17

For generations, the City of Hot Springs practiced a form of government allowing its leaders to be elected to lead and represent an area where they refused to reside. This was legal in Hot Springs and in many parts of the South. Because of the limited influence possessed by African Americans in their community, they often vented their problems and needs through their elected officials.

An advocate for the mayor-alderman form of government, Beard opposed the manager-board form of government because he felt it didn't allow as much involvement of the community with its elected officials. Each election, Beard campaigned on a platform of overcoming racism because he wanted to create an atmosphere for the community to openly discuss what he viewed as a sickness that people always tried to avoid discussing. Once he made his point in the campaigns by protesting the system and receiving a certain amount of ink in the press, he always felt victorious.

**Elmer Beard, front row right, at an annual Arkansas Power & Light Company meeting with Hot Springs city officials in 1971**

Before he donned a three-piece suit working inside the system, he was a 1960s civil rights activist. As a new member of **Roanoke Baptist Church** in Hot Springs, Beard got involved in the church and the community under the leadership of the Rev. James Donald Rice. Beard joined forces with Rice as they worked to integrate public facilities and institutions in Hot Springs, including the public schools. This social agitation led, many believed, to the "mysterious" fire that destroyed the historic church that was founded by ex-slaves and their slave masters. A long-time deacon, he continues to serve on the trustee board and sings in the male chorus at Roanoke.

ELMER BEARD, YOUR Metropolitan Insurance Salesman Contact him for all your insurance needs at 503 W. Grand or call 624-5544: Evenings, 624-6806.

**1973 newspaper ad**

His career as an alderman prepared him for his future. It was a balancing act to handle politics on one side and a career in education on the other, but he managed. After earning a bachelor's degree in English from Arkansas Baptist College in Little Rock and a master's degree in education from Henderson State University in Arkadelphia, he worked as an educator teaching students from grade school to the university level. He also worked as an insurance agent in Hot Springs at Metropolitan Life, selling policies to many members of the African American community. Beard was an ambassador on the Hot Springs Chamber of Commerce and a member of the Democratic Central Committee.

For Beard, politics was a family affair. His father, Luther Beard, was an alderman and school board member in his hometown of Chidester during the 1980s. His nephew

19

LaVelle Peete became the third generation of his family to serve in public office when he was elected to the school board in Decatur, Illinois. Beard also had local family support for his political interests. Beard's late wife of 40 years, Dorothy, a native of Marvell, would often check their three children—Morris, Phyllis, and Sonya—out of school to campaign at the polls on Election Day. Years later, his second late wife, Wilhemina, a native of Beloit, Wisconsin, was a supporter of his political activity.

During Beard's tenure, he challenged the city council to modernize undeveloped and underdeveloped neighborhoods with an infusion of essential public works programs. Those calls for improvement were welcomed, and he continued to issue new challenges for the city leaders to maintain the upkeep of the neighborhoods.

Fellow *Challenger* Junius Stevenson, left, and Elmer Beard

Here are some of the proposals Beard initiated during his 16 years on the Hot Springs City Council:

- ✔ Addressed abandoned houses, vacant lots, and undeveloped streets
- ✔ Proposed the installation of public facilities for neglected areas of the city
- ✔ Petitioned the city to close Chattanooga Street Dump and develop a city park in 1972
- ✔ Hounded news media and reported illegal dumping in Ward 3
- ✔ Requested city street lights, speed limit warnings, and neighborhood watch signs
- ✔ Secured funds to develop street paving, drainage system, and neighborhood parks
- ✔ Solicited more than $725,000 for public works projects from 1972–1976
- ✔ Recruited minority contractors to bid on public works projects in Ward 3
- ✔ Lobbied to hire the city's first black fireman amid opposition from the fire chief in 1971
- ✔ Sponsored ordinance to ban loitering on public parking lots and residential streets
- ✔ Initiated annual residents meeting of constituents with an agenda for Ward 3

The retired eight-term Alderman Elmer Beard has lived to see each of these proposals become a reality. Beard became one of the most experienced African Americans in the history of Hot Springs politics. Unlike many others in his socioeconomic class, Beard still lives in Ward 3, always a man of the people.

# Alfred Bedford

The decade of the 1970s saw more African Americans running for public office than any previous decade. In 1971, Alfred Bedford was one of them. He ran for the school board in Hot Springs. With 282 votes, he finished in fourth place out of four candidates who ran, according to *The Sentinel-Record* on September 21, 1971.

This was a school board election so he ran at-large, as did all the board candidates. Had he run by district like the recently reformed city government that had changed to a one-man, one-vote system, he would have had a better chance at winning.

Bedford, a native of Ouachita County, was a World War II veteran. When he returned home from the service, he entered the **Spa City** bathing industry, where he worked until he retired. He and his wife, Iola, raised three children. One of his daughters, Dorothy Jean Young, taught school in the district.

According to his daughter Helen George, he was a hard-working, friendly guy who loved his family and his church. He served in several positions at St. Paul A.M.E. Church on Garland Avenue in Hot Springs. Feeling the need to extend his leadership skills beyond Sunday services, the one-time candidate for public office solicited support from his family and from leaders in the black community. His campaign was a motivation to those who knew him, especially former Alderman Theodore "Pootie" Page, a fellow officer in his church. He contacted the NAACP Unit 6013 to endorse his candidacy, and the officers were eager to get out the vote.

# William E. Bonner

William E. Bonner was a barber and a tutor for student barbers. He was born in McCrory, a rural town near Newport, in northeast Arkansas. Bonner moved to Hot Springs when his son, Herbert, was 3 years old.

Bonner filed for public office repeatedly during the 1960s, according to records at the Garland County Clerk's Office. He also was part of the unprecedented four black men who ran for alderman in 1968, adding local political heat to what had been a year of national protests. Bonner's bids were unsuccessful. However, he made a political statement each time he filed for office by showing that he was willing to challenge the system.

Bonner had worked as a clothes presser, and he also was a successful businessman. He established the first professional barbershop of his generation for black residents in Hot Springs. He, like a good father, became his son's first teacher; the son, Herbert T. Bonner, was his apprentice and heir to his business. Later, Herbert, who would become an icon in the business community, always credited his father for his success. The business was in continuous operation for 63 years.

Politics often were discussed in Bonner's Barbershop. He would encourage his clients to register to vote and get involved in the community. Bonner had the support and respect of the local citizenry. He was a minister of the gospel and an associate pastor at the Roanoke Baptist Church. His faith, politics, and business success became a part of the rich history of his adopted city, Hot Springs.

# Herbert "H.T." Bonner

Herbert T. Bonner, or "H.T." as he was called, followed right in his father's footsteps, becoming a successful barber and political candidate.

Back in 1964 and 1966, Bonner ran unopposed for justice of the peace, according to the Garland County Clerk's Office. Bonner understood the political pulse of the system, and particularly, the pulse of the black community. One of his reasons for running was to instill pride in his fellow residents. He wanted his customers and people in the community to follow him in his activism, and many residents did. His father, William, also ran for public office in the 1960s, making H.T. the second person in his family to go into politics. The father-son duo were among the first political dynasties in the making in Hot Springs.

**Herbert Bonner with wife Dorothy**

His daughter Petrella Bonner-Pollefeyt said she had preserved an old certificate that Bonner received when he was a justice of the peace. It was signed by the late and infamous Arkansas Governor Orval Faubus, who is best known for blocking the nine black students from desegregating Little Rock Central High School in 1957.

Serving as a justice of peace was time consuming, but Bonner never let anything interfere with his profession,

**Black students attended the segregated Langston School, 1903-1969.**

his craft of barbering. He had taken over as owner and operator of his father's barbershop, which had remained open for 63 years and had become an institution in the black community. Like the atmosphere in his father's shop, it was a place where politics could be discussed.

Bonner was a 1939 graduate of the segregated Langston High School in Hot Springs. During that time, Langston was considered to be one of the top all-black high schools in the state. Bonner was elected president of the Langston Booster Club and was a co-founder of the still celebrated and well-attended Langston High School reunions.

In addition to being of the Methodist faith and active in his local community, Bonner was gregarious and supported many worthy community projects, including hosting social gatherings at the end of each year to show his appreciation to his many customers.

Bonner died in 2003 at the age of 82.

# Birdie Boyd

Birdie Boyd and her husband, the Rev. Clarence Boyd, were the only African American husband-wife duo to serve in public office in the City of Hot Springs.

**Birdie Boyd**

In 1977, Garland County Judge Bill McCuen appointed Birdie Boyd as justice of the peace. "There weren't many blacks in community service at that time, so I thought it would be a good opportunity."

In addition to politics, Boyd served as **first lady** at Visitor's Chapel A.M.E. Church, where Rev. Boyd was pastor. She wrote a popular etiquette book for pastors' wives titled, *So You Want to Know, Don't You?*

Boyd studied at Oklahoma Langston University in Langston, Oklahoma, and then at Henderson State College in Arkadelphia, where she received a B.A. in English and a minor in French. She also earned a master's degree in education from Henderson.

She served as a justice of the peace until her husband's position as a pastor required them to relocate from Hot Springs to Little Rock. Boyd spent her career as an elementary school teacher in the Hot Springs and Pulaski County school districts.

She also was active in the community here. In 1977, the local chapter of Gamma Phi Delta Sorority, a professional black women's organization, invited Boyd to address its members at a function. A strong supporter of the sorority, Boyd, one of her daughters, and two of her granddaughters all became members of Gamma Phi Delta.

# Rev. Clarence V. Boyd

The Rev. Clarence Boyd, a prominent **African Methodist Episcopal** pastor, was as involved in the community as he was in the church.

In 1980, Boyd was appointed to the Hot Springs School Board Position 2, by board members. He completed an unexpired term; he then ran unopposed for election and won a seat on the school board. When his term was completed, he did not seek re-election.

Rev. Clarence V. Boyd

When he wasn't holding office, the Rev. Boyd was the state director of the Workforce Incentive Program, working with women in need. Until Boyd retired, he was a full-time minister; for many years, he pastored the historic Visitor's Chapel A.M.E., which was the largest church in its denomination in Hot Springs.

Like his wife, Birdie, the Rev. Boyd was active in the Gamma Phi Delta Sorority, serving as vice-president of the Cavaliers, its male auxiliary. He often offered the sorority the use his church fellowship hall for fund-raising events.

Known for his impeccable diction, Boyd had a command of any situation. A cross-section of people in both high and low places paid him the greatest respect. He continues to live the life about which he preaches and still has a lasting impact on the black community to this day.

The Boyds were the only African American couple to be appointed to public office in Hot Springs. They now reside in Little Rock.

# Cedell G. Briggs

In a January 1983 article of *The Arkansas Citizen*, Cedell Greathouse Briggs was listed as a candidate for

Position 1 on the Hot Springs School Board.

At that time, she and her husband, John, had one child who was 17 years old and attending high school. They were also the parents of four other children.

In the article, Briggs joined Alderman Kenneth Adair and other black community leaders in asking any resident who

**Cedell G. Briggs**

was not registered to vote to exercise their constitutional right and let their voices be heard by registering to vote. This resulted in an increase in voter registration that was largely due to her efforts.

This was her only attempt to run for public office. She was defeated for Position 1 during the March 1983 election.

Briggs worked tirelessly as a faithful member of the Cottrell Chapel **Christian Methodist Episcopal** Church. In her professional life, she was employed as an instructor and interpreter at the Hot Springs Rehabilitation Center, according to *The Arkansas Citizen.*

Briggs served as secretary of the NAACP Unit 6013 prior to running for election to the school board. The NAACP supported Briggs in her run for the school board position, and she later served as president of Unit 6013.

# Annette Butler

Annette Butler won her first campaign for Position 2 on the Hot Springs School Board in a March 1987 election, according to records in the Garland County Clerk's Office. Butler won the race 462–352 over James Kallman and was re-elected in 1990, according to *The Sentinel-Record.*

Butler moved from Alabama to the Spa City and wasted no time rolling up her sleeves to improve the local school district.

She supported the campaign to restore the former Central Junior High School building, which was the old senior high school of President Bill Clinton. The board had to decide carefully on its preservation and use for historical purposes. In its

**Annette Butler**

restoration of the building, the board retained the original design of the interior and colors of the early 1960s.

The magnet school concept was new to educators and school directors in the district. They had to examine and experiment with this new concept in education. Butler was aware, as were the other board members, that without the magnet school practices in the Hot Springs School District that enrollment would continue to plummet. Butler was a part of the district that faced reality and continued to provide the best education for the district's children. Once Superintendent Roy Rowe commented that he wished he had an entire board as competent as Butler.

She became president and led with enthusiasm. Her influence was contagious. At least one local resident, Vicky Anderson, was influenced by her leadership and became a candidate for a position on the board.

Butler observed measurable growth within the school district and was an involved parent. She had that magnetic persona and exhibited qualities that made it an honor for the NAACP Unit 6013 to support her candidacy.

# John Clayton

In the general election of 1984, John Clayton and incumbent Elmer Beard were opponents for Ward 3 alderman. Clayton gave Beard a close race, according to the Garland County Clerk's Office: The final vote count was Beard, 619; Clayton, 544. This effort to defeat seven-term Alderman Beard was one that gave Clayton his first round of positive press in the political arena.

The position held by Clayton that helped to prepare him for this close race was on the 10-member board of directors of the **Spa Development Corporation** (SDC). Although he didn't create the corporation, he was its strongest spokesman and cheerleader. Clayton got the idea for getting involved in the development corporation from Darcy Dobson. Clayton and Dobson met while selling tip sheets at the Oaklawn Park racetrack. In later years, Clayton and Dobson became board members, stockholders, and officers of the SDC.

In 1984, the NAACP Unit 6013 applauded Clayton for his persistent efforts and courage to partner with Dobson to preserve the historic National Baptist Hotel and Bathhouse.

**John Clayton with daughter Audria**

In 1983–1984, each stockholder would invest about $300 with an option to purchase the Baptist Building in six months' time, pending necessary financing. The inability to obtain funding would lead to the demise of the SDC. Clayton took his position very seriously, said Dobson. Clayton and the SDC members had a vision and were truly committed to restoring the famed African American hotel. They were unified in that one mission. During the efforts to prevent the hotel from being demolished, Clayton was campaigning for a position on the city council. Being able to say that he was a stockholder in the National Baptist Hotel and Bathhouse was a powerful plank in Clayton's political platform. He was a member of CLOB and the NAACP Unit 6013.

Clayton's nickname was "Sweat," which he earned for his outstanding performance as a football player for the all-black Langston High School. His teammate and Darcy's brother, Gary Dobson, explained that "Clayton would hit you so hard, it would make you sweat!" Clayton was known to be aggressive both on and off the playing field.

Although Clayton had just one campaign for political office, his campaign to save the National Baptist Hotel and Bathhouse was a success in that the Baptist building was not demolished. Darcy Dobson managed the necessary paperwork to create the SDC, and Clayton kept the public focused on the potential of the National Baptist Hotel and Bathhouse, and this important contribution was a crucial step on the long road to its restoration.

The history was also preserved. During the **Jim Crow** era, the Baptist building was one of the largest black hotels in the state. It was once home to annual meetings of the National Baptist Convention, USA. Attracting the biggest names among the black elite, its guests included tap dancer Bill "Bojangles" Robinson, who was at the time the highest paid black entertainer in the country. The Negro League baseball players also stayed there. After integration, the black hotel could no longer compete and closed its doors.

Today, it is a modernized apartment building.

Clayton fought to preserve the historic National Baptist Hotel and Bathhouse for years. This photo was taken by John J. Archibald.

# Mattie L. Collier

Mattie L. Collier requested and preferred everyone to call her Mrs. T. J. Collier.

In 1970, Governor Dale Bumpers appointed her as an original member of the Board of Trustees of the Garland County Community College, now known as National Park College. Her term expired December 31, 1976, according to county courthouse records. Collier was re-elected without opposition in the November 1976 election. Due to her declining health, she resigned in December 1978.

**Mattie L. Collier**

33

Collier's presence on the board of trustees was felt during her tenure. In a 1973 interview, Collier said she and Alroy Puckett approached community college President Gerald Fisher about hiring black faculty members.

The epitome of professionalism, Collier worked as an elementary teacher, counselor, and a principal. She once referred to counseling as her first love in education. Having been a counselor at Langston High School, she later became principal at Goldstein Elementary School, where she served until she retired. She lived four blocks from the school.

Collier graduated high school from Arkansas Baptist College in Little Rock. Education for blacks developed very slowly across the South. For example, black folks' school terms were usually shorter than white folks, which was why she earned a high school diploma from a college. Also, she earned a bachelor's degree from the same school but since Arkansas Baptist was not recognized by North Central Association of Secondary Schools, that degree needed to be certified at Bishop College in Marshall, Texas, through additional coursework. Collier earned her master's degree at the University of Arkansas in Fayetteville.

Though Collier grew up during a time when educational opportunities were inferior for black students, she still excelled at Arkansas Baptist College, Bishop College, and University of Arkansas in Fayetteville.

She recalled with joy how she received the highest-ever score on a University of Arkansas at Fayetteville graduate entrance test. The exam was changed after that, she said.

Collier grew up as an only child and lived somewhat of a sheltered life. She met Torrence J. Collier at Arkansas Baptist College. They were married, and he became a doctor. The couple had one son, Torrence J. Collier Jr., who himself later became a doctor of public health.

In society at that time, two distinct differences existed. It was common for most whites to talk *to* rather than talk *with* blacks during the Collier era. By contrast, blacks were expected to say "sir" and "madam." Black women almost always experienced a lack of respect. Collier and others in our educational and social circles recalled being called "boy" and "girl" until they were into their senior years. After that they were referred to as "aunt" and "uncle." The disrespect and inequality of blacks, especially black women, were common during Collier's youth and adulthood. Collier protested this mistreatment until she received her due respect.

Collier was Baptist. Those who knew her at church and at work recalled her being as "meticulous as they came." Once she was traveling with Elmer Beard and his family. Beard washed his face at a rest stop, and he left it wet so he could stay alert. Collier couldn't endure the sight of his dripping wet face as he returned to the car. For her sake, she insisted that he dry his face with a tissue provided by the meticulous Mrs. Collier while Beard's family watched in silent awe.

With Collier's grace, intellect, and poise, she had an impact on those who knew her. She appeared determined to change and challenge the social norms during her lifetime. One of the factors in her husband becoming a medical doctor was to earn a title and the respect of his family, friends, and associates.

She never apologized for preferring to be addressed as Mrs. T.J. Collier rather than Mrs. Collier. Whether you liked her or not, you respected her as Mrs. T.J. Collier.

# Joyce Craft

In November 2000, Garland County voters elected Joyce Craft to a six-year term on the Board of Trustees for Garland County Community College, since renamed National Park College. She ran for re-election in 2006

and was elected. She ran and was elected for a third term in 2012, according to college records.

The Cotton Plant native would be the fifth African American elected to the college's board of trustees. In a 2013 interview, Craft said she observed too few black employees hired at the college, during her 12 years of serving on the board of trustees. The sta-

**Joyce Craft**

tistics from the NAACP revealed only about 10 percent of the student body was made up of students of color, and the organization encouraged African American students and professionals to seek admission to or employment at the college.

At her day job, she was able to make great strides in diversity in education. Craft made history becoming the first African American to serve as superintendent of the Hot Springs School District. Unlike many of Craft's predecessors, she possessed these impressive qualifications for leadership: double majors in business and English, experience as a high school teacher, and an administrator in the Hot Springs School District. Craft received her bachelor's degree from the Arkansas Mechanical and Normal College, now the University of Arkansas in Pine Bluff, and her master's degree from Henderson State University in Arkadelphia.

Her work ethic and professionalism has been superb in every aspect of her performance related to her work in the school district. Craft began her tenure with the Hot Springs School District in 1972 as a language arts teacher. Within the district, she later taught Advanced English and Computer Technology. Her qualifications for advancement and promotion were apparent to the district. As an assistant administrator, she learned the policies and practices of the school system. "I did not get to where I am alone," she said, in remarks made during a celebration in which she was honored in 2013.

Long-time school district official Ted Nobles said of Craft, "Joyce is the most organized superintendent that I have worked with in my more than 40 years in District 6." Nobles further pointed out that she had excellent communication skills with her colleagues and staff. School board President Joe Reese noted Craft's exemplary service in all areas of administration that she had been assigned.

Craft and her late husband, Frank Littleton, are parents of two children, Dierdre Littleton Shead and Attorney Levell Littleton, both graduates of the Hot Springs School District. The doting grandmother of four is currently married to Lieutenant Colonel Curtis B. Craft Jr., and both attend the historic Roanoke Baptist Church.

She is a role model among her peers, her elders, and the younger generation that will follow in her footsteps.

# Rev. William T. Davis

In 1998, The Rev. William Theodis Davis ran for Position 2 on the Hot Springs Board of Directors. He was one of four candidates but lost the election. Davis' other political experience was as one of three representatives on the Garland County **Election Commission**. He was the only black ever to serve as a commissioner.

**Rev. William T. Davis**

His most newsworthy contribution to the community was his presidency of the NAACP Unit 6013 during the late 1980s and early 1990s. Davis called a news conference of the local NAACP in front of the historic National Baptist Hotel and Bathhouse building in August 1989.

According to the local CBS affiliate, KTHV-TV News, Davis had filed a suit against every school district in Garland County to prevent the loss of more white students from the Hot Springs School District. The goal was to preserve integration in the face of **white flight** to the outer districts during the school year.

The outcome of the lawsuit was a federal court order that required parents who requested to change the school district of their children to present a utility bill with the new legal address in order to validate the move. Without the court order, parents were free to remove their students at will, and this would have threatened the ethnic diversity of the school district.

During his stint as NAACP president, he hosted the city's first Dr. Martin Luther King Jr. Parade. Davis solicited various government agencies to participate. Two decades later, the parade continues under the sponsorship of the board at the **Webb Community Center.**

Davis had unintended difficulties in his time as president of the local NAACP. He expressed great hardship convincing local ministers to use the pulpit to organize and advance the community. It was a challenge for him to lead the chapter while he was pastor of a congregation 100 miles away at Union Grove Baptist Church in Gould. If he had been pastor of a local church, he felt his results would have been more effective.

However, Davis' heart was in Hot Springs. During his tenure as NAACP president, a black resident was shot by a white police officer who claimed the victim pulled a gun on him. Davis was labeled as the black community's leader by the media. Meetings were held to smooth relations, but Davis was unable to garner support from the community. Still he persevered, and eventually the policing of the housing projects improved after the shooting.

A veteran of the U.S. Air Force, the Rev. Davis retired as supervisor for the Buick Division of the General Motors Corporation. He is a seminary graduate and a licensed minister in Michigan and Arkansas. Davis and his wife, Mary, still reside in the city; his son and stepdaughter are graduates of the Hot Springs school system.

# Sharon Delph-Mohammed

In the September 2002 Hot Springs School Board elections, Sharon Delph-Mohammed ran for a three-year term. She had a close race, according to the Garland County Clerk's Office. Drew Stonecipher received about 52 percent of the votes; Delph-Mohammed received almost 48 percent of the votes.

Delph-Mohammed, who had just moved her children from a private school to the Hot Springs School District, said her primary concern was the quality of their education. That prompted her to run for the school board position. Also, she was motivated by the negative response she received from teachers and administrators. "I witnessed students who were graduating and unable to read or write at their grade level! And the resounding answer I got from school officials was, 'We can't reach them all!' I couldn't accept that answer, and I wanted to see a change in what I describe as a defeatist attitude," she said.

The government should make public school education one of its top priorities, Delph-Mohammed said. "The future of Arkansas and this nation depends on ensuring that all children receive a great quality of education ... and school boards are the first line of defense to ensure that a great quality of education comes from the schools they represent," she said.

Delph-Mohammed advised any aspiring candidate to be fully committed and mindful that all students deserve someone who will lobby on their behalf. School officials have a mighty task, she said, adding, "Many have gone before you and submitted to the notion that our children cannot learn and or be taught. This, friend, is a lie!"

Effective school boards play a vital role as watchdog. More specifically, Delph-Mohammed said she believed administrators should keep local schools on track for the success for all students, setting the vision and goals for the school district, developing policies that affect current and future students, holding the district accountable for teaching, and ensuring that all students have a fair and equitable chance for a great education. She stressed during her campaign that these mandates would be regardless of the child's ethnicity or religion.

"Although I realize that as one school board member I couldn't change the culture or policies alone," Delph-Mohammed said, "I could be effective as a board member by working with other school board members."

The best outcome came from working in collaboration, she said, when members blended their unique gifts and talents. The message Delph-Mohammed wanted to send was that when school districts make teaching and learning their business, it gives students a fighting chance, she said. "These kids could live out their dreams because they were ready to meet the challenges of today's world."

# Robert Easter

In the September 1989 election, Robert Easter filed to run for Hot Springs School Board Position 2. He finished in fourth place of four candidates, according to the Garland County Clerk's Office. This would be his only effort to seek public office.

There was a constant need for African Americans to be represented, so Easter stepped up to the plate. He and his wife, Mavis, a political science major and social studies teacher, had two children attending schools in the district.

Easter, who worked at the Hot Springs Rehabilitation Center, was accustomed to catering to clients with special physical, mental, or emotional needs. His professional experience caused him to recognize the need for a vocational education curriculum for students with learning disabilities. The educator and counselor had the support of the NAACP Unit 6013 when he announced his candidacy; his campaign was ignited by former local NAACP President W.T. Davis and the 1989 lawsuit against each of the seven Garland County school districts.

Without the NAACP's legal involvement, this rich diversity would never exist today. The Hot Springs School District became the only Garland County district that developed various magnet schools that created advanced specialized curriculum. While the NAACP was supportive of Easter, it was limited in what it could do for him, and he received little help from the community. However, Easter left his political mark in what became a more diverse and modern school district.

When Easter retired, he moved to Little Rock. He has one daughter who lives in Hot Springs.


# H.H. "Chick" Ferguson

Career businessman H.H. Ferguson completed the necessary paperwork for city alderman twice, in 1956 and in 1968, according to *The Arkansas Citizen*. He was unsuccessful in both bids.

In 2012, Ferguson had but one surviving relative still

living in the area who knew him. She was his cousin Jean Almore of Hot Springs Village. The National Baptist Hotel and Bathhouse on Malvern Avenue included space for Ferguson's business, Almore said. Ferguson worked full-time in the transportation business as the owner and operator of a taxi cab.

To obtain a ride in a white-owned cab was rare at that time, so black-owned cabs were necessary. Ferguson knew the schedules of the trains and buses arriving at the stations in Hot Springs. Upon arrival at the train station, "The drivers would approach African American visitors, take their luggage, and carry them anywhere they wanted to go for 50 cents," said retired Hot Springs Police Sergeant William Watkins.

The pulse and the rhythmical sound of the political community were appropriate each time he ran for city council. Ferguson foresaw a change coming. As a businessman, he wanted to be a part of that change. Each time he made a run in his cab, he was acutely aware of the business impact of his efforts. Chick got a sense of what was going on in the community, of the things that needed changing and or improving. Ferguson would set his mind on remedying the situation.

In 1956, he could afford to be an alderman, which came with a salary of $30 a month. Being self-employed, Ferguson could control his work and schedule, and he was be able to attend council meetings. He and other businessmen in the black commercial district of Malvern Avenue supported each other.

When Ferguson ran for city alderman in 1956, he was a resident of Ward 5. During the at-large system in use prior to 1970, Ferguson knew his chances of success were limited. Yet, he paid his $1 filing fee and obtained the required signatures to get his name printed on the ballot, according to the Garland County Clerk's Office. In the election bid, he won the majority of the votes in his ward but lost in the total vote count to the white candidate.

Undeterred, Ferguson was one of four African American candidates who filed for alderman in Hot Springs in the elections of 1968. The other city council candidates were Theodore Page, E.S. Stevenson, and Raymond Tweedle. Kenneth Adair, also a black businessman, filed for the position of city clerk. Though each candidate lost the election that year, their campaigns made a statement.

These failed election bids went a lot further than mere attempts to run for public office. Their efforts were never in vain. Becoming a candidate gave each man more exposure in the city while drawing on the strength of the growing civil rights movement and civil unrest nationwide.

Ferguson didn't run again. He had name recognition, however, and continued to ask residents to register to vote. Ferguson and other businessmen in the Malvern Avenue district paved the political path to the one-man, one-vote system adopted in 1970. As of that year, candidates ran for election from a particular ward.

The community knew him as "Chick," a man to whom they could call on as needed. All during those years, Ferguson was a secret member of the NAACP trying in his own way to be an organizer for change. "Many of us are still standing on his shoulders to this day," said *Challenger* Elmer Beard. The local NAACP and CLOB never forgot his path-paving contributions for others to follow.

# Nathaniel "Bob" Freeman

In April 1998, Nathaniel Freeman was appointed to the unexpired term of Harriel White on the Hot Springs School Board, according to the school district records. Freeman later ran for school board in September 2001 and was subsequently elected, according to the Garland County Clerk's Office.

**Nathaniel Freeman**

In a recent interview, Freeman said that there was a last-minute change in polling place locations during his campaign. The original location was the Webb Community Center, where a majority of black residents voted. The unexpected change in polling places would have drastically reduced the number of African American voters. Even with the last-minute change, he was still able to rack up 70.6 percent of the votes cast. The only other black candidate on the school board, Birkes Williams, said that he attributed the success of the campaign to flooding the community with flyers. Freeman, who is now serving his fourth term in office, agreed.

Freeman, a soft-spoken North Carolina native, came to the Spa City when his company transferred him. When he wasn't working his nine to five job, he was making an indelible difference as a school board member. In fact, he is credited with leading the way for some historical first in the Hot Springs School District, particularly when it came to hiring African Americans in leadership positions.

Freeman had a major role in the appointment of former teacher Joyce Craft becoming the assistant superintendent. In 2007, Freeman brought to the attention of the school board that Craft was classified as assistant to the superintendent and not as the actual assistant superintendent. "This was a surprise to some of the board members," Freeman said. The injustice was soon corrected.

Later on, Freeman was instrumental in the promotion of Craft becoming the Hot Springs School District's first African American superintendent.

Freeman with student Tamira Brown

A vast majority of the school board members voted for Craft's promotion. He was also very instrumental in the hiring of the first African American head football coach at the high school. He was on the interview committee and presented his recommendations to the board members, and they supported his decision. In 1999, the board selected Alfred Mohammed, according to school district records. Freeman and the other board members believed that an African American head football coach would be "a positive for the school," Williams said, considering the diverse pool of student athletes.

These experiences showed his ingenuity and experience. Freeman, who had worked with employment practices in his career over the years, was the only board member with personnel management expertise. He served long enough in his years on the school board to see the injustices of racial discrimination reversed—and to become the man on the board who made the difference.

Freeman is a graduate of Norfolk State University in Norfolk, Virginia. His bachelor's degree is in business with an emphasis in marketing and personnel management. Freeman brought to the school board invaluable and necessary experience. He and his late wife, Veronica, had one daughter, Natalie, who was a product of the Hot Springs School District.

This loyal servant is a member of the historic Roanoke Baptist Church, where he serves on the Deacon Board and is a member of the finance committee. In addition to fighting battles here in his community, he served his country for two years in South Korea.

Former NAACP president Elmer Beard remembers attending a crowded school board meeting and taking a seat on the floor. Beard recalled then-Superintendent Roy Rowe commenting, "Maybe we should have charged a fee tonight." Freeman, offered a more noble gesture. "He got up from his seat and found me a chair," Beard said, adding that it reminded him of the verse Matthew 25:40, "Inasmuch as you have done it unto the least of these ..." Among colleagues and friends, Freeman has often been described as the definition of a true gentleman.

# Belinda Gaines

Belinda Gaines moved to Hot Springs in 1991. As the mother of two, she saw a need for her services in the district where her children attended school. She was a strong supporter of the school's extra-curricular activities. She promoted an equal and quality education for all students.

Working the concession stand at football games wasn't enough to satisfy Gaines' desire to become involved in the public schools. She thought that her attitude and the attitudes of her children's teachers should always be positive, motivating, and encouraging. She and her husband, John, took pride in their attendance at all the parent-teacher conferences.

In 2002, Gaines ran for school board in Hot Springs. She ran a good campaign but lost to Robert Kleinhenz, according to county courthouse records. In her professional life, she has proven her business savvy in the insurance field. Also, she and her husband operated a fish market for more than two years. Though she didn't win her race, she left a political imprint in the school community.

# Hermas Gant

Hermas Gant became candidate for Garland County Quorum Court Justice of the Peace in the fall 1970 general election. He had no opponent and was sworn into office in January 1971, according to county courthouse records.

The retired Reynolds Aluminum Company employee had a heightened sense of the needs of the community. His first step in giving back was that of a notary public. As a member of Eureka Baptist Church, he became an officer and later accepted his calling to the ministry by serving as an associate pastor at his home church.

Gant was an active member of the Masons and an involved member of the Olive Branch Lodge. After being a lodge member for many years, he then decided to launch his first bid for elective office by running for justice of the peace. Though he only served one term, he is still recognized in the black community for his courage in running for office during a time of barrier-breaking.

# William Gant

William Gant, a proud father of four, often said, "When it's all about your kids, parents ought to be involved."

In 1977, his desire to help his community motivated him to run for the Hot Springs School Board. He was unsuccessful in his bid for this office, according to county courthouse records. Gant tried again but lost another run for school board in Searcy, he said in a 2015 interview.

A native of Helena, Gant graduated from Lane College in Jackson, Tennessee. He served as pastor at Cottrell Chapel C.M.E. Church of Hot Springs and other Arkansas churches. He often encouraged the participation of more African American parents in the schools, urging them to be "role models for their own children."

His family life, his ministry of the gospel, and his community involvement stayed steadfast throughout his career. Supporters and church members admired how he reared four children mostly on his own. They grew up and are all degreed, employed, and making a positive contribution to society.

# Bertram A. Garmon

In 1986 and 1994, Bertram Garmon ran for the Hot Springs Board of Directors, according to records at the Garland County Clerk's Office. Each bid was unsuccessful.

**Bertram A. Garmon**

A Prescott native, Garmon ran for city director because he wanted to make a positive difference here in his adopted hometown. Alderman Kenneth Adair encouraged him to be proactive, working within the political system to help or change the issues that he opposed in the system. Garmon, a husband, father, and grandfather, found time to give each campaign his best effort. He often said he believed too few young men in their 30s and middle ages showed little interest in their community.

As an educator and a musician, he led a colorful career. Garmon's degrees and certifications were commendable. With his academic ability and critical thinking, his ideas and proposals created some tension in the public education arena: He questioned why it was a general practice that coaches often advanced to administrative positions and leadership roles. Garmon, who had an issue with the practice, believed his credentials as a math teacher made him just as, if not more, qualified for those positions. He later became the superintendent of the Walker School District in Columbia County, he mentioned in a 2014 interview.

For more than four decades in education, he attended several workshops in order to stay current in the latest trends, innovations, practices, and policies in the field of education. Garmon said the success of schools is contingent on adequate funding for programs that address the needs of students and policies that are student-focused. Beyond funding, he also said that both administrators and parents could drastically transform the quality of schools. "It will be accomplished with a dedicated faculty and staff who show students they care and are able to find ways for all students to experience success," he said in a 2014 interview. "The involvement of parents and the support of the community will ensure the success of schools."

Garmon was a member of one national organization, four state professional organizations, and a fraternity. Yet he had time for his church work at the historic Visitor's Chapel A.M.E. Church, where he served 18 years as a choir director. He always made time for sharing his talents with the church community. During his years as an administrator in Magnolia, he served as an organist for St. Phillip's A.M.E. Church.

He also participated in the United Way of Columbia County, and he was a member of Abilities Unlimited, Inc. No votes or campaigns were necessary for Garmon to develop an appreciation for his philosophy of education. His students and scholars were the winners and living proof of the success of his guiding principles. "I believe schools should provide the opportunity, resources, and an environment where all students will learn."

# James "Jim" Godfrey

James "Jim" Godfrey initially served in the positions of college administrator and professor. In 1999, he served on

**James R. "Jim" Godfrey**

the Board of Trustees at the Garland County Community College, renamed the National Park College.

Employees usually do not advance from a salaried position or staff member to board member. Godfrey did just that. "I served for several terms before my business required me to travel extensively, at which time I had to regrettably vacate my board position," Godfrey said. He served on the board from November 1994 to December 31, 2000.

Godfrey pushed for an increase in enrollment of students above and beyond 1,300 to 1,500 students. In fact, he saw the enrollment grow from 1,500 to more than 3,000. On his assessment he believed the enrollment increase was achievable, and it happened.

Other records of Godfrey included his encouragement and outreach of the college to aid and assist the minority community with initiatives like health screenings, tutoring sessions, and job fairs administered through the Webb Community Center. To do so would connect the college with diverse segments of the neighborhoods that were often unintentionally overlooked. "I encouraged the pursuit of combining the college and the technical school," Godfrey explained, always thinking about the future of education and students.

He supported upgrading a computer system and also improving the science laboratories. Godfrey influenced Joyce Craft, his Leadership Hot Springs classmate, to run for a board position. Craft, like most of the other African American board members of the then-Garland County Community College, ran unopposed.

Godfrey, an alumnus of the segregated Langston High School, brought class preparation and professionalism to the board of directors. He earned a bachelor's degree from Pepperdine University, in California, and is a veteran of the U.S. Air Force. His career encompassed positions with General Electric, Installations and Service Engineering, higher education administration, and business ownership. Godfrey has served in many positions, including as one of the most effective presidents of the board in the history of the Ouachita Area Council Boy Scouts of America headquartered in Hot Springs; Godfrey also sponsored and supported several successful community programs.

Godfrey is a former board member of the Webb Center, where he proposed various programs to form alliances with the community college and the community center. This bond, he believed, was a great investment for both institutions. Godfrey is proof that black elected officials need to caucus from time to time, and he is a testament to how elected officials need to get behind each other in much the same way that he mentored Craft.

# Aaron Gordon

Aaron Gordon ran for office four times. He lost three elections, and one time, he wasn't even aware that he was actually running.

Ironically, his greatest political victory did not involve a political race of his own; it was a court case. In 1993, Gordon sued the Garland County Election Commission over **gerrymandering**. Based on U.S. Census records, it was revealed that the division of wards and distribution

**Aaron Gordon with wife Gloria**

of voters resulted in no black-majority districts in Hot Springs.

The NAACP Unit 6013 filed the suit on behalf of Gordon; the lawsuit alleged that the current boundaries discriminated against the city's black electorate. In 1994, a judge ruled that the lines had to be re-drawn. In light of the ruling, the city scheduled a special election in March 1994. Now running in a race against three other African Americans, Gordon would lose the bid for Hot Springs Board of Directors to the lone white candidate, Pat McCabe, in District 2, according to November 1993 records at the county courthouse.

The election came with one catch. To ensure that the board of directors would have some returning members as opposed to a board of all newcomers, directors had to pull straws. A long straw meant a candidate would serve the full four-year term. A short straw meant a candidate would serve nine months and then seek re-election to complete the remainder of the four-year term. McCabe pulled a short straw, so he had to face Gordon in November 1994. This time Gordon won, according to county courthouse records. Gordon would serve the remainder of the four-year term on the board of directors for District 2. During his term, he was appointed as vice mayor of the City of Hot Springs.

In his 1998 bid for re-election to the board of directors, Gordon was defeated by *Challenger* Elaine Jones.

Then unknown to him, he was running for a seat on the Hot Springs School Board. Aaron Gordon didn't choose to run on his own, he was **drafted**. Bob Hansen, a member of the Central Democratic Committee, distributed campaign materials before Gordon filed to run. "Friends put up campaign signs with my name on them, without asking me. Finally I talked to my wife and ended up running for the school board," Gordon said. He lost the election.

In 2000, he made his final attempt at office in a run as District 2 Justice of the Peace on the Garland County Quorum Court, according to county courthouse records. This was the open position previously held by the recently retired Justice Alphonso Logan. One other candidate, Thomas Anderson, also filed for the District 2 Position. Gordon contended that Anderson may not be qualified to run based on his residency. A review and then a vote of the Garland County Central Democratic Committee ruled that Anderson was in compliance with the rules.

Gordon credited then-Alderman Elmer Beard with

jump-starting his interest in politics. Beard took Gordon to register to vote at age 17, so he would be eligible to vote in the first election after his 18th birthday. "I started getting informed and going to board meetings," Gordon said. His political career took flight.

When Gordon wasn't politicking, he was in the pulpit. Gordon never expected to become a preacher, he said in an October 1977 interview for *Citiscape*, a newsletter for Hot Springs city employees. "When I was saved 22 years ago, I began dedicating myself more to the church. I don't like crowds, and believe it or not, I am on the shy side. But God called me to preach, so I went to theology school and became ordained." To learn the ropes, Gordon drove more than 140 miles round-trip three times a week to pastor a church in Nashville for more than six years. In 1992, he opened the Water of Life Church of God in Christ (COGIC) in Hot Springs. Recently, it merged with the Angel Gabriel COGIC, where he is now senior pastor.

Though he spent his time helping the community and saving souls, Gordon's day job was as manager of the Majestic Bathhouse. Residents remembered, however, that for 40 years, Gordon has been a voter, a candidate, and the go-to man for political struggles in his community.

# Gary Gordon

The first time two African American brothers ran for the Hot Springs Board of Directors was in the 1980s. They were Aaron Gordon and Gary Gordon. Gary was the younger brother.

In the spring of 1985, Gary Gordon was a young father. A memorable image from the campaign trail was how

Gary's wife carried their newborn child in her arms. It was a touching family affair.

Gordon, a disabled U.S. Marine veteran, filed as a candidate for city director in District 2. Another candidate, Elijah Harris, was the winner of that election, according to the Garland County Clerk's Office. This election was in the first round of elections for city director following the change to the city manager form of government.

Gordon worked at the Majestic Hotel and Bathhouse. His supervisor was his older brother, Aaron Gordon. Gary asked his brother, Aaron, to run for city director in District 2. "I became his campaign manager," Gary Gordon said.

The Gordon brothers experienced some political pains. During a lull in leadership in the black community in Hot Springs, Gary influenced his brother, Aaron, to file a lawsuit for the NAACP Unit 6013. Aaron Gordon had argued that the balance of wards across the city should have Ward 2 as a majority-black district; it was a majority-white ward. While the judge hearing the case didn't rule in favor of Gordon, he agreed that it should be a black-majority ward.

In 1993, after the case, the Garland County Election Commission members re-drew city ward boundary lines to avoid protests. Commissioners also re-drew the lines specific to Ward 2.

Despite the vote count, Gary Gordon was a winner then and now. He now lives with his wife in Los Angeles, California, where he works for the federal government.

Even out of office, the Gordon brothers were a political force of nature. They managed to right a wrong in the system and the electoral process that had stifled black candidates running for office for decades.

# Albert M. Harris

One of the standout up-and-coming leaders of the community is Albert Harris. His only experience in a run for public office was a Hot Springs School Board position in the election of September 2002. Debbie Ugbade won the election, although Harris managed to capture about 29 percent of the votes, according to the Garland County Clerk's Office. The position was for a three-year term.

Harris, one of the city's most outspoken critics for the diversity deficit on the Hot Springs Police Department, has questioned the racial inequity as well as the gender inequity on the force. The Hot Springs High School graduate has more than 22 years of leadership experience under his belt. A soldier on and off the battlefield, he has been described as a self-motivated self-starter with a "skill set of intelligence, information, technology, and military training," which were instrumental in his drive and success. Harris has been a part of high-level security operations in the military that he cannot discuss publicly. But he is proud of his service to his country and now focuses on making a difference in the community.

The one-time school board candidate lists his civilian education as spokes in the wheel of progress toward his retirement as a lieutenant colonel in the U.S. Army. He has a bachelor's degree in liberal arts from Henderson State University in Arkadelphia. He also has a graduate certificate as Chief Information Officer. He is a fifth-generation minister of the gospel. Harris, who is single, is a property owner in the historic Pleasant Street neighborhood. He is encouraged by the progress made in his community where his ancestors laid a foundation.

# Elijah Harris

In the new form of government in June 1985 Elijah Harris was one of the first members of the Hot Springs Board of Directors. Harris, who served on the Visions in Action Task Force, made an enduring mark in history as the city's first African American to serve as mayor.

His political career began in 1985, when he defeated Gary Gordon for director of District 2, according to the Garland County Clerk's Office. Harris continued the necessary meetings with residents in the district that had been successful in previous administrations under the city council system. This was very important in the mid-1980s with the new form of government. During his 1986–1987 term, Harris announced the borders of District 2: "District 2 has irregular, difficult-to-describe boundaries. It includes most of what was previously the Third Ward on the near eastern side of the city, plus an area on the near southeast side extending to the eastern edge of Jaycee Park, and an area to the northeast of downtown that includes the eastern section of Whittington Avenue extending north to the Glade Street vicinity," he explained in a 1987 interview with *The Sentinel-Record*.

District 2 has always had special needs. Harris directed his interest and attention to those needs with the $200,000 grant he supported for low-income housing. Although he hoped for $500,000, this was a good start. "We have to cut back, way back, on what we are trying to do. There is a big difference between improving 20 houses instead of 50 houses," he said in the article.

As housing conditions improved, Harris continued to lead the Visions in Action group. This was a task force

# The Claus Connection

In the midst of the Christmas crunch, Santa needs the counsel and thoughtful perspective of individuals who do not rush to judgment, who do not make rash decisions under fire, who speak with the voice of reason.

Santa searches out those who have a strong sense of self, but are willing listeners and keen observers, those who can stay the course in the midst of turmoil and in the aftermath of success.

Santa wants on his sleigh persons fully committed to whatever the task at hand may be, men and women unafraid of taking risks and confronting problems.

Santa feels particularly pleased about his selection of **ELIJAH HARRIS**, city director, as newest member of the St. Nick Society.

Elijah Harris, manager of Business Service for Arkansas Power and Light Co., comports himself with poise and professional elan, even under the most trying circumstances.

Elijah Harris, whose community involvement extends to Little Rock as well as in his hometown of Hot Springs, is man who speaks his mind clearly and carefully, a man who can make tough decisions in a non-abrasive manner, one who can bring sensibility to a debate and assurance of resolution to seemingly impossible situations.

The Sentinel-Record

created to advance and improve Hot Springs. It was composed of elected officials and local residents. It had short- and long-range goals. Many residents had their input in the goal-setting guidelines for the city with these results: The committee addressed issues of economic development, transportation, downtown revitalization, quality of life, public safety, and financial resources.

In 1987, then-Executive Editor Melinda Gassaway of *The Sentinel-Record* featured him in her popular Christmas-time biographies called the "Claus Connection." Of Harris, she wrote he "comports himself with poise and professionalism, even under the most trying circumstances."

Although the goals of the task force didn't specify detailed needs of African Americans, there was one issue that Harris directed with skill, art, and poise. In the late 1980s, some residents requested renaming Gulpha Street to Dr. Martin Luther King Jr. Street. City government didn't often change street names. It would take 75 percent of city council members to be in favor of a street name change for that to happen. The matter went to a committee and then to the city council.

On the night of the vote, two board members were absent. In a skillful move, Harris voted to dissent. This forced the issue back into the hands of a committee for re-evaluation. Otherwise, the issue would have died in the council meeting, and that would have been the end of the issue at that point in time. Harris' dissent kept the issue alive by referring it to a committee.

In the end, instead of a short street tucked away in an area less traveled, a greater victory came as the result of Harris' shrewd judgment. On August 21, 1989, Resolution

2441 was adopted to rename the U.S. Route 270/70 around Hot Springs as the Dr. Martin Luther King Jr. Boulevard. A further step was taken on July 1, 1991, when Ordinance No. 4146 was adopted by the Hot Springs City Council to rename the U.S. Route 270/70 around Hot Springs as the "Dr. Martin Luther King Jr. Expressway."

There also was other significance to Harris' vote. A generation earlier, the local NAACP had fought for the opportunity to have a diverse city council. Harris was the right man for the right time. He was aware that with low city board attendance, the issue could have been lost.

Harris became the assistant city mayor after being elected a director. He had to assume the duties of mayor when Mayor Jon L. Starr resigned during his ninth month due to moving out of the city for personal reasons. Harris and City Attorney David White contacted the Attorney General's Office seeking advice about Starr's replacement. Until a successor for Starr was found, Harris presided over the board of directors as the acting mayor and worked with the city manager with political decorum. Harris had the support of White, other members of the board of directors, and the local NAACP. He served until an election was held when Helen Selig was elected, but he will go down in history as the first African American to serve as mayor of Hot Springs.

Harris served for many years as a business manager at the Arkansas Power & Light Company, where he retired. He and his wife, Helen, are members of the Roanoke Baptist Church, where he serves as a deacon. He is also a member of Roanoke's finance committee, which is in the process of rebuilding the historic church.

# Illean A. Harris

Following her retirement, Illean Allen Harris filed for a position on the Hot Springs Board of Directors, according to records from the county courthouse. Her bid was considered a great effort by her former principal, Mattie L. Collier.

Harris would receive a reasonable number of votes and made a strong political statement. It required courage for an African American woman to run for office. When she ran, she lifted up her neighborhood. The career educator was influenced by Margaret L. Martin, both were good neighbors, dedicated educators, and stewards of the Baptist faith.

Illean A. Harris

Harris was a native of El Dorado, where she attended public schools. She received a bachelor's degree from the Arkansas Mechanical & Normal College, now known as the University of Arkansas in Pine Bluff. She spent many years teaching at Goldstein Elementary School. At one time, she was a member at Greater St. Paul Baptist Church, and at another point she was a member of the historic Roanoke Baptist Church. Harris died at age 84 in 2007. She and her late husband, James E. Harris, left a son, Terry, and four grandchildren.

# Hovey A. Henderson

In December 1978, Hovey A. Henderson was appointed to the Board of Trustees of Garland County Community College, now National Park College, according to the board of trustee records. Henderson was appointed by the board after original member Mattie Collier resigned. Four years later, his term would expire. Professor Henderson, as he was popularly known by his students, served those four years with another original board member and fellow *Challenger* Alroy Puckett.

**Hovey A. Henderson**

Born April 18, 1911, Henderson was a 1929 graduate of the segregated Langston High School. He earned a bachelor's degree from Arkansas Mechanical and Normal College, now the University of Arkansas in Pine Bluff, and a master's degree from Atlanta University in Georgia. He was a teacher and principal at Langston Junior and Senior High School until 1970. Henderson was inducted into the Hall of Honor of the Hot Springs School District in 1988.

The son of a Baptist minister, Henderson was a well-versed and talented musician. For more than 50 years, he served as the organist of the Visitor's Chapel A.M.E. Church. His equally gifted brother John Henderson was the popular organist at the historic Roanoke Baptist Church.

64

# Kezel Holmes

A veteran of World War II, Kezel Holmes was stationed in the Philippines. When he wasn't on the battlefield, the Hope native was living an active life here in his home state of Arkansas. After he graduated in 1946 from the famed Langston High School, he married Vertie Lee Bullock, and the couple parented six children.

**Kezel Holmes**

Holmes later moved to the East Coast living in Philadelphia and in Pemberton, New Jersey. There he had a diverse work history, which included establishing the Holmes Food Center, a community grocery store. A successful businessman, he also owned an auto repair garage. In addition, he worked many years as a parking lot supervisor at the Children's Hospital in Philadelphia and as a bailiff in a Philadelphia Court until he retired in 1988.

In 1963, Holmes was called to the ministry of the gospel. He became an ordained minister and founded the Clearview Baptist Church in the early 1970s. He later served as an associate minister at the Pauline B. Grant C.M.E. Church in New Jersey.

He was also a Past Master of the Masonic Order "Pride of Ethiopia" Chapter 104. Among Holmes' hobbies were gardening and photography. In the late 1980s, Holmes returned to Hot Springs in District 2, and he registered to vote in November 1989.

"He met no strangers. He loved the public and the pulpit," said the Rev. Leon Massey. Holmes, as Massey recalled, was also remembered as a talker and politically proactive. Holmes filed for director of District 2 in a special election of March 1994. There were two black candidates, Aaron Gordon and Bert Garmon, and one white candidate, Pat McCabe, who vied for the same position. The winner was Pat McCabe, according to county courthouse records.

In the next election of 1994, Holmes worked to help Aaron Gordon defeat McCabe, Gordon said. Holmes, the newcomer to campaigns in Hot Springs, supported Gordon wholeheartedly. When Gordon won, Holmes felt like a winner, too. Holmes died on October 1, 2013, at age 87.

# Edwinor Horton

Edwinor Horton was the first African American woman to vie for the Hot Springs School Board. She filed to run in a March 1970 election but was defeated by veteran member H. Dale Cook for the position, according to the Garland County Clerk's Office. The Hot Springs native, was the second black woman to file for public office in the city. Margaret L. Martin was the first.

Horton was born December 10, 1910, to the parents of Marshall and Elizabeth Puckett Whitmore. According to her obituary, she was a charter member of Haven United Methodist Church and was very active in church work, serving in various capacities before her health failed. She also was a charter member of the social club Entre Nous.

On November 11, 1942, Horton married Joe Cephus

Horton of Alabama. The couple met while she was a student and a teacher in Alabama. Her vocation in Hot Springs was as a clerk at Bernett's Jewelry Store on Malvern Avenue.

While her candidacy was low-key, much like she was, the need for African American female candidates became a reality, especially on the school board. Horton, like many of the other African American candidates, won in her ward and precinct during the 20th Century. Her mere campaign created an unmeasured pride and respect for her in the community. Winning in one's own precinct was a victory.

# Willie Huff

Willie Huff was a candidate for the Hot Springs School Board, in 1974 and 1976. He lost both times, according to the Garland County Clerk's Office.

Huff always wanted better for himself and others. He would jokingly refer to his neighborhood as the "rejects" as opposed to the "projects." He disclaimed it to encourage other residents to outgrow the projects because he was successful moving out of the public housing. An Arkansas native, Huff attended the all-black Langston High School and Arkansas Mechanical and Normal College, now the University of Arkansas in Pine Bluff.

He worked in the hospitality and hotel service industry. His later years of service were spent with the Community Service Organization, where he later retired. Huff was known to be very good at leading and following as the opportunities availed themselves.

He was widowed in recent years and now lives with one of his children in Northwest Arkansas.

# Gladys Ivory

Gladys Duvall Ivory ran for the Hot Springs School Board Position 2 in 1972. She lost to Richard H. Wooten, 1,507 to 377, according to county courthouse records.

She was known in her community for being a leader on various issues, such as getting roads in the Chattanooga Park area paved. She also was relentless about getting the city to connect homes in that area to city water and sewer.

Ivory was born on March 26, 1921, in Hot Springs and attended public schools. She and her husband, Bennie Lee Ivory Sr., were parents of Bennie Jr. and Lonnie. Ivory, who was serious about the need for young people to be properly educated, was an active parent in her children's education at their black catholic school, St. Gabriel's.

**This Sentinel-Record photo shows Gladys Ivory at the polling place.**

By profession, Ivory was a beautician. She was also very active in her community in social clubs like Entre Nous and in her church, Eureka Baptist. She was described as being a dynamic public speaker and often made her rounds speaking before local congregations.

Ivory, an accomplished soloist who performed at various events around the city, even won an Amateur Night at Harlem's famed Apollo Theater in New York City. She went on to record a gospel album. She died in 1987.

# William "Moose" Jackson

William Jackson, known as "Moose," filed for alderman in Ward 3. In the 1976 election, he placed fifth out of the five candidates, according to county courthouse records.

A Hot Springs native, Jackson was a star basketball player at Langston High School. While working at a local restaurant in Hot Springs, he was recruited and attended college in Oklahoma. When he returned home, he shared some of his basketball experiences with local youths.

He served with the U.S. Air Force in Vietnam between 1965–1970, before being honorably discharged. He left the armed forces a disabled veteran and continued to give civilian work his best effort. The local NAACP considered it a stately move when he applied for and was hired by the Hot Springs Police Department working for a short stint as an officer. Few blacks were employed on the force at that time.

He called Eureka Baptist Church his home, said his sister, Mary Ruth Goshen. Jackson died in 1979 at the young age of 39.

# Elaine Jones

Dreaming of running for public office in 1994, Elaine Jones was encouraged by family and friends to run in 1998 for Hot Springs Board of Directors District 2. She did so and won her first campaign and has been re-elected three times. She defeated incumbent Aaron Gordon when the first of her four terms began after the election in 2000.

**Elaine Jones**

Jones followed Aaron Gordon on the Hot Springs Advertising and Promotion Commission. The position allowed the local NAACP and constituents more access and use of the Hot Springs Convention Center. The convention center is in proximity to the Webb Community Center, which is the heart of the social and political meeting place in the black community. Ever since the construction and extension of the Hot Springs Convention Center, the city director for District 2 has served on the Hot Springs Advertising and Promotion Commission, a dire need that was practiced since Gordon's terms in office from 1994–1998. "I saw a lot of things I thought I could accomplish with the people's help," Jones said.

Much of her time is divided among other organizations. Jones is actively involved with the Webb Community Center, where she has been a member for more than 30 years. She unashamedly refers to the Webb Center as "her baby." Her leadership skills at the center helped to spearhead her campaign for her first election to the city directors. Jones has always been enthusiastic about the future of the community center. "I feel like this is really important work. We have to keep the center going and growing," she said. Jones also serves as secretary of the Pleasant Street Neighborhood Association.

In addition to her love for all things Webb Center, she has a special place in her heart for the National Baptist Hotel and Bathhouse. During her tenure as city director, she has taken a strong stance when it comes to preserving the historic building on Malvern Avenue. While some of her colleagues and constituents grew tired at the failed attempts to reopen the building, she jumped to the defense. As one contract called for residents to move in the Baptist building by the end of the year, a fellow city director commented, "No one wants to live there." Jones responded, "I'll live there if it's necessary." Her willingness to relocate temporarily would have honored the contract.

She and her husband, Chester Jones, have been married for more than 40 years and have a blended family of a son and a daughter. Jones is a native of Jennings, Louisiana, and while her roots are there, her heart is in Hot Springs.

---

## DID YOU KNOW?

Of the 63 candidates studied, Jones won the two closest races. In 1998, she trumped Michael Smith by 21 votes, according to a 2007 report at the Garland County Clerk's Office. In 2010, she bested Willie McCoy by fewer than 30 votes.

---

# Alphonso Logan

Alphonso Logan served as a Garland County Quorum Court Justice of the Peace for more than 20 years. He never had a serious opponent. At the end of his last term

**Alphonso Logan**

in 2000, Logan, then 92, was one of the oldest serving elected officials in Arkansas history, according to the Secretary of State's Office.

This characterization was a mere snapshot of Logan's long career, according to an excerpt in his obituary: a military and civilian instructor, a coach, a businessman, and a counselor were "experiences which contributed to his wit as well as being outspoken on issues he felt strongly about, even sometimes casting the only dissenting vote while serving on the court."

Logan and his twin brother, Alonzo, were born to Eloise and Abraham Logan on August 15, 1908, in Hot Springs.

After his public school education, Logan attended Knoxville College in Tennessee, where he double majored in math and science. He also had been a teacher and a football coach. Upon graduation from college in 1929, he returned to Hot Springs and obtained employment as a coach and math teacher at the segregated Langston High School. He developed state championship teams that were supported by both communities, black and white. Two members of his teams played in the National Football

League. Later, Alphonso and his wife, Dorothy Logan, coordinated the Langston School reunions. The reunion has hosted more than 700 graduates and former students from across the nation and abroad. It's a proud tradition that still continues to attract alumni every other year.

As a scholar of science, in his later years, Logan developed a serious interest in model trains. His interest in trains could have started while working on the Canadian Railroad as a Pullman porter, a position known to be held by black men during that time.

In the early 1980s, one of the major issues of Logan's tenure on the Garland County Quorum Court was re-districting. Today's **voting rights** activists voice some similar concerns Justice Logan expressed in *The Sentinel-Record* in December 30, 1981:

- Redistricting would result in having seven new members out of 13 on the quorum court who knew nothing about county government.

- Gerrymandering would result from redistricting and diluting the black vote in the city's Ward 3 and the county's District 9.

- The new boundary lines would violate the 1965 Voting Rights Act.

Logan was joined by other officials in the redistricting meeting. Aldermen Kenneth Adair and Elmer Beard were the most vocal proponents of the Voting Rights Act. All elected officials present were opposed to the Garland County Election Commission de facto gerrymandering.

With cooperation from the elected officials present, the black district remained intact. This was one of the many struggles of the black elected officials in Garland County. Logan was and remains the first and only African American to be asked to administer the oath of office to an elected official. Logan gave the oath to County Judge Bud Williams because the judge had been absent when the other newly elected officials of an election year took their oaths of office. This was a great honor to Logan and was very much celebrated in the black community.

**Alphonso Logan with wife Dorothy**

"He was known for keeping a watchful eye on affairs that affected his constituency and the betterment of his race," Dorothy reflected about her late husband in his funeral program. Logan died December 23, 2002. He was 94 years old.

---

## DID YOU KNOW?

Langston High School was a major reason African Americans moved to Hot Springs at the turn of the 20th Century. Hot Springs was one of the few cities in the state that offered a quality high school education for black students.

# Rev. Perry Lomax

The Rev. Perry Lomax ran for public office twice in Hot Springs. He made unsuccessful attempts for city alderman and city director. His greatest contribution to the community involved him making the city safe.

Before Lomax even launched his first bid for office, he started working in the system to make a difference. He was extremely saddened to hear about a fatal car wreck just outside of the city limits on U.S. Highway 70 East, in the westbound lanes. The 1975 car crash claimed the life of a Hot Springs School District guidance counselor. Lomax figured that something had to be done to prevent this tragedy from happening again. He investigated the crash site and designed a safety measure by creating a turning lane at an angle. The Arkansas State Highway and Transportation Department implemented his recommendation.

Rev. Perry Lomax

Then Lomax found politics. Often he would seek the advice of then-Alderman Kenneth Adair. One occasion, Adair recalled how Lomax consulted him about unseating a black alderman in the 1976 election. Lomax believed that the alderman was too passive for the community. He contended that the city councilman should be more outspoken like Adair. Lomax was reminded by Adair that each politician had his own style of governing to achieve similar goals. Lomax lost the election to the incumbent.

The second time the Rev. Lomax ran for office was for the position of city director in 1983, according to the Garland County Clerk's Office.

The Starkville, Mississippi, native came to Hot Springs with his mother at the age of 13. Lomax began working at the Southern Grill and Club for 50 cents an hour, he said. His father was a building contractor for the Mississippi Highway Department.

Lomax's formal training included studying at the Hot Springs Rehabilitation Center, the Jackson Theological Seminary, and Shorter College. His studies at the Hot Springs Rehabilitation Center prepared him to become a certified nursing assistant, which provided him training he would apply to his work in a nursing home. He was the first black to be employed by Lockwood Men's Store as a salesman. He worked in several motels, and in 1991, he became the dining room manager at the Derby Dinner Theater in Hot Springs.

The Rev. Lomax has practiced three different religious denominations. He was called to preach as an attendee of the Baptist faith. Later, the **African Methodist Episcopal Zion** Church licensed him to pastor. Then he became a United Methodist minister.

In the 1960s, the Rev. Lomax was active in the local NAACP, recruiting new members and serving on the advertising committee. During the struggle to elect the city councilman by ward, Lomax was always involved. Though he never won public office, Lomax goes down in history for making Hot Springs a safer place for people traveling in and out of the city.

# Fred W. Martin

Fred Martin was one of the first black elected officials in Arkansas during the Jim Crow and **poll tax** era. He was sworn into public office in January 1955, according to the Garland County Clerk's Office.

Martin was born in 1896. According to Tom Hill, curator for Hot Springs National Park, a great deal of information remains on file about Martin's career as a bathhouse attendant. Martin had to pass a physical, work, and mental exam before going to work in 1923; he scored 100 points on those exams, Hill said. During his long career, Martin worked at both the Arlington Hotel and

Fred W. Martin

Maurice bathhouses, but he spent most of his employed years at the Arlington Bathhouse.

Martin was moved to become active in civic life in Hot Springs. Little did he know that his decision would lead to city, county, state and, eventually, national prominence. The 1954 U.S. Supreme Court verdict in *Brown v. Board of Education of Topeka, Kansas* and events of that year led Martin and others to decide that there was finally going to be a change in local politics. In the fall of 1954, Martin filed and ran for city alderman. Martin felt that if public schools were to be desegregated that the city council also should be desegregated.

A very interesting turn of events happened in the city council elections of 1954. Fred W. Martin and Clifford

## Negro Attends Demo Rally, 40 Whites Leave

*Martin*

In Little Rock, Ark., a group of about 40 segregationists walked out of a state Democratic Party dinner and fund-raising rally after they learned Fred W. Martin, 63, a Negro state Democratic committeeman, was present in the audience of about 600 persons. The group's spokesman, Rev. Wesley Pruden, angrily charged that Martin's presence at the $10-a-plate dinner was a deliberate attempt by integrationists to "try to embarrass us." The rally featured guest speaker Sen. Sam J. Ervin Jr. (D., N.C.) and Gov. Orval Faubus.

Martin was featured here in *Jet* magazine in April 1958.

Martin appeared on the same ballot but from different wards. Fred was black, and Clifford was white. After Fred W. Martin was elected, many white residents who voted for him said they meant to vote for Clifford Martin because they thought Fred W. Martin was the white candidate.

At the county courthouse the next morning, many tried to change their vote, according to a janitor who was an eyewitness and shared with Fred Martin what he saw. Martin, some years later, relayed the information to Elmer Beard. The peer pressure by residents upon the county clerk to change the vote results didn't work. That event never made it into the newspaper that day either. To report the mix-up would have indicated that whites were not ready to desegregate. They wanted to appear advanced beyond that, while at the same time trying to deny blacks a duly elected seat on the city council.

Martin is known for more than having broken the color barrier. During his two-year term, he recommended that each city council meeting begin with prayer. This practice ceased during Mayor Dan Wolf's administration. Mayor Tom Ellsworth resumed it, and the tradition continues to this day. Without one demonstration or any protest from the black community, by virtue of being elected to public office, Martin's victory began the desegregation of Hot Springs city government.

Tom Ellsworth

In 1954, aldermen were paid an **honoraria** of $30 a month for their service. Martin would receive that payment throughout his two-year term in office.

In hopes that he could be re-elected, Fred Martin ran in 1956 against Ralph Wright, a white businessman, but lost. Martin ran again in 1957, unsuccessfully. In 1960, Martin ran against Wright one last time and although defeated, Martin won in Wards 2 and 7. In short, Martin ran and won; then he ran and lost, ran and lost, and ran and lost.

There is one photo of Martin known to exist. It appeared in an April 1958 edition of the *Jet,* a national news weekly magazine, covering issues affecting black people.

Of note, in a review of voting results, every black man who ran in his city ward or county district between 1954–1970 won the most votes in his home ward.

His legacy remains to this day. Fred W. Martin had influenced Hot Springs, Garland County, and Arkansas history. He advanced the clock on race relations, and because of him there was no going back.

# Margaret Long Martin

Margaret Long Martin was the first African American woman to win public office in Hot Springs. She was also the only black woman to run for three different political positions; they were school board member, justice of the peace, and city director.

**Margaret Long Martin**

She was a candidate for justice of peace several times, winning each election. This was at a time during 1954–1970, when candidates for the justice of the peace had no districts and no opponents. The positions weren't salaried during that time, but the justices did receive a small stipend. Back then, there was one justice of the peace for every 200 residents.

Martin ran for the Hot Springs School Board and served from 1975–1976, according to records from the Garland County Clerk's Office. Serving with her at that time was another *Challenger* Garland Puckett. This was the first time two African American members were on the school board at the same time.

Martin also was a candidate for city director in District 1; she lost that election in March 1986. Long-time alderman Elmer Beard remembered Martin as a woman who was determined to be first in everything she did. "In her 1986 effort, I posted her campaign sign in my yard along with 13 other candidates. Martin visited the display of posters and moved her poster from the center of the second row of signs and placed her sign front and center," Beard recalled, as if Martin was daring him to make her second to anyone. Martin commented to Beard, "Now, everyone will be able to see my name."

It was always fun when she ran for office, Beard reflected, adding that if people did not know Martin well, she could be intimidating, despite her lack of height.

Martin prepared herself for public life as a scholar at the segregated Langston High School. Then she graduated from Knoxville College in Tennessee, and the University of Arkansas in Fayetteville with a bachelor's degree and a master's degree respectively. She matriculated at other higher educational institutions, where she continued her studies throughout her career.

The historic Roanoke Baptist Church was where she was reared, baptized, and trained in the tenets of the Christian faith. When Martin returned from college as a young teacher, she held at least five different positions over many decades at the church.

She was a proactive member of the NAACP. She joined during the period of time when it was common for the NAACP members to carry their membership card in their shoe for protection.

As an elementary school principal, a high school English teacher, and a university instructor, she left a long-lasting impression on all of her students. While she studied for many years, she encouraged her students to do likewise. Her education and political history is a legacy others would want to emulate. In fact at her home-going celebration, many of her students gave their best impersonations of Mrs. Martin. She lived to be 101 years old.

# Willie J. McCoy

After a recount in the general election of 2010, Willie James McCoy lost to veteran City Director Elaine Jones by 29 votes, according to the Garland County Clerk's Office. This was his first attempt at running for public office.

**Willie J. McCoy**

McCoy said the local government should represent the best interest of the community. "The residents of Hot Springs have become frustrated and disappointed with city government, and the buck stops with the city directors," McCoy explained as part of his political agenda. "Hot Springs is ailing from a lack of community-oriented leadership in city government. Hot Springs needs to be healed from the inside out."

In the Jones-McCoy matchup, Jones was going to run for her fourth term. During her third term, she had contacted McCoy about serving on a committee or board in city government. It would have been a resume-building qualification for McCoy. Instead, McCoy decided to challenge Jones. McCoy lost and Jones was re-elected.

A decorated veteran, McCoy recalls being interviewed by the promotion board in the military. He was asked: "As a leader and supervisor what is more important to you, the men or the mission?" In the military, it's the mission, McCoy answered. Ask that question in city government and the answer is often the men—or, in the city's case, personnel. However, McCoy said, the city gets that answer wrong; it should focus on the community welfare. "Hot Springs needs a city government that is mission-focused. It's not about giving residents what some department heads think they need. This is about giving what is deserved. It's a basic, government for the people." McCoy has had a lifetime of focusing on the mission.

He is among five generations to serve his country in foreign conflicts. He served two tours of service in the Vietnam War from 1968–1971 and earned awards including a Bronze Star for Meritorious Achievement in Ground Operations against hostile forces. Returning home, he pursued a career in law enforcement. Early in his career, employees were offered educational opportunities through the civil service. McCoy took full advantage of this.

Professionally, he climbed as high as the system allowed him to climb—he received two associate degrees, one in criminal justice and one in sociology from Garland County Community College, now National Park College, between 1979–1980. He then went to Henderson State University in Arkadelphia, where he received a bachelor's degree in social work in 1983 and a master's degree in community counseling in 2000. Four degrees made him one of the most academically qualified police chief candidates in the history of the Hot Springs Police Department. Yet he lost the job to a less academically qualified applicant. Though McCoy had his sights on becoming police chief, he retired from the force as a captain.

A police officer should live within the city limits where that officer works, McCoy suggested. "City government needs to become pro-Hot Springs. More effort should be put into hiring personnel to live in and become a part of the Hot Springs community," he said. McCoy's most recent position was patrol division commander, also the chairman of Internal Affairs. In addition to being a patrol officer, he worked as service division commander and shift and patrol division lieutenant.

He also suited up for the elite SWAT Team. McCoy stayed involved in the community as a member of the Board of the Boys' and Girls' Club. A four-time Arkansas heavy-weight amateur boxer, McCoy coached younger fighters in the ring. He also has been active in the Friends of the Parks and an alumnus of Leadership Hot Springs. As a member of the St. Mark Baptist Church, he is chairman of the trustee board and president of the Brotherhood, a missionary organization. At home he is husband to Janice, a school administrator, and father to six adult sons.

When he wasn't in police uniform, McCoy worked for two major corporations, Reynolds Metal Company and Weyerhaueser. He also taught part-time at the National Park College. Off the clock, he invested time developing plans to fix what was broken in Hot Springs.

The Spa City could use a boost in the promotions department, McCoy explained: "City government has done a poor job of representing and selling Hot Springs as a safe and quality place to live for all residents, especially new employees at both ends of the pay scale."

A self-described fighter for the people, McCoy recalls a staffer being fired for wearing a mascot cap of an opposing team to a meeting. Many organizations take a strong stance on commitment, said McCoy, adding, "It's all in or get out." Elected officials need to be true stakeholders in city government, he said. "Your heart is where you live."

# Rev. Fred Nicholson

Since moving to Hot Springs in 1978, the Rev. Fred Nicholson has had no idle time. In addition to being a family man, a pastor, and community leader, he had to balance a successful career with Entergy, formerly known as Arkansas Power & Light Company.

**Rev. Fred Nicholson**

He was a deacon in his local church and became a teacher of deacons in the Southwest District of the Baptist State Convention in Arkansas. Nicholson said that he was befriended by the Rev. Clarence V. Boyd and Alderman Elmer Beard when he first came to Hot Springs. Deeply involved in his church, he felt that serving his community was an extension of his church's mission.

In 1988, after 10 years of living in the city, he filed for a vacant position on the school board, according to the Garland County Clerk's Office. Encouraged by his friends and neighbors, Nicholson was able to win the close race.

Twice re-elected and along with other board members, he was able to initiate many new educational programs in the district: new state standards for schools were implemented; computer technology courses were newly created, and teacher testing was state-mandated. Nicholson was also able to help keep the schools desegregated. He was supported by his fellow board members.

To serve his community was a rewarding experience for Nicholson who had children in the district. He saw and felt the needs of the students, including his own. For example, some school buildings didn't have air conditioning. He supported this improvement. When Nicholson considered not running for re-election the second time, Superintendent Roy Rowe encouraged him to give it one more term, stating that he was needed more than he realized. Although Nicholson had a close race in his first election, he had strong support from his church and the black community. Nicholson's philosophy was that his debt to the district was paid when he no longer had children in the district. Consequently, when his children graduated, he practiced his philosophy and did not seek re-election.

The Rev. Nicholson serves as co-founder of Emmanuel Christian Fellowship Church, which focuses on Christian education and community involvement. Nicholson is a living example of the sermons he preaches. His work as a member of the school board is still appreciated.

# W. Clarence Nolen

W. Clarence Nolen felt indebted to his adopted city. The Mandeville native lived a life of community involvement and church leadership for many decades. His family followed his commitment and interest in public service.

As a candidate for city council in 1976, he was defeated by Alderman Kenneth Adair. The vote count was Adair with 1,064 votes to 462 for Nolen, according to county courthouse records. Nolen was appointed to the Hot Springs School Board before he ran in 1978, according to school district records. He later ran for Hot Springs School Board Position 1 in 1979 and was defeated by Melinda Baron 492–417, according to public records.

When Adair learned that Nolen had filed for the position, he made a personal visit to discuss the matter with him at Nolen's office. They had a cordial conversation. However, Nolen continued in the race and was Adair's only opponent from the black community.

For many years, Nolen was employed in service work. He served as chairman of the Webb Community Center Board of Directors in the late 1960s. He later worked for the Employment Security Division in Hot Springs, where he was able to help many of his fellow residents find gainful employment.

Leadership Hot Springs, not the same organization that is active today, was organized by Nolen. It was a community forum that lasted two years. Many residents were informed about the community regarding its civic opportunities and services available to residents. The main goal of Leadership Hot Springs was to bring fair and equal opportunities in housing, education, employment, politics, and fair business practices for all members of the black community. Nolen made himself a major force in the progress toward unifying all residents of Hot Springs.

He was a family man with three daughters who attended Langston High School. An enthusiastic member of the Langston Booster Club, he was involved in all areas of their academic progress. A Baptist by faith, he was a member of the Union Baptist Male Chorus, and later became director of music there. His dedication and work for his church was an essential part of his life.

# Theodore "Pootie" Page

Theodore "Pootie" Page operated Page's Mortuary for more than half a century. During this time, the Hot Springs native served just one term as city alderman in Ward 3, from 1971–1973.

Page had run for the position three times in the 1960s during the at-large system of electing city councilmen,

**Theodore R. "Pootie" Page**

according to county courthouse records. His campaigns showed the injustice of citywide elections during segregation. Based on his repeated attempts, the NAACP and CLOB had proof that supported his claims and those of other black candidates that the citywide at-large system was racially biased.

An at-large system allows a candidate to reside in one ward and to be voted on by residents from every ward. In 1970, four white and three black candidates filed to run for alderman in the new Ward 3. Page was one of those candidates, according to *The Sentinel-Record*.

Page and Alderman Elmer Beard had the two highest votes of the seven candidates, and both won in Ward 3. "Pootie," as many people knew him, stopped by Beard's home on the day after the race and congratulated him on the election to office of city councilman.

In 1972, Page ran for re-election but lost to Kenneth Adair, according to courthouse records. After the election, he said he wasn't interested in making politics a career. He said if he could serve two terms, he would have given the position to Adair. Page was never given the opportunity to hand over the throne. During his one term in office, however, Page was able to serve his constituents with class and character.

The Langston High School graduate was also a World War II U.S. Army veteran and a graduate of Gupton Jones College of Funeral Service in Decatur, Georgia. He was a mortician and funeral director for Page's Mortuary in one of the many businesses that his father owned in the black commercial district on Malvern Avenue.

While operating the funeral home, he also was involved in several organizations, including the Webb Community Center, the NAACP Unit 6013, Chamber of Commerce, the National Funeral Directors Association, Golden Gate Masonic Lodge No. 48, and The Knights of the Pythias Fraternal Order. He also was a historian and archivist.

Campaign advertisement from *The Sentinel-Record*

He was the youngest offspring of William and Minnie Ash Page, pioneers and trailblazers in the black business community; Alderman Page's family had been in Hot Springs for several generations and was one of the oldest black families in the city. He was married to Ernestine Rosborough for more than 58 years, and they had one daughter, Harriet Edelhart, of Las Vegas, Nevada.

Page's brother-in-law, Ross Rosborough Sr., lived right next door to him. They were not only neighbors, they were also political opponents in the 1970 election for alderman. Rosborough Sr. finished in fourth place; Page finished in second place, winning a seat on the council.

During the 87 years of his life, Page witnessed more changes in Hot Springs than most residents. For example, an irate white resident used the N-word in a city council meeting while explaining a problem he had with large trucks, transportation, and the black neighborhood. This happened in the council chamber in 1971. Page's reaction was, "I haven't heard that word in public for a long time!" Page and all the other aldermen were uncomfortable with the language. Some residents later apologized.

As a member of the Public Works Committee and Public Health Committee, Page was an active participant in their endeavors. He was able as an alderman to influence the planning committee to approve the relocation of Page's Mortuary on Pleasant and Silver streets. Since its existence, it had been located in the business district on Malvern Avenue. He was a strong supporter of peace and progress in city government. He would serve as an example of the struggles and successes of black candidates.

# Leonard "L.C." Pettis

Of the 11 candidates filing for mayor in the November 1970 general election, Leonard "L.C." Pettis finished the race in seventh place. During the campaign, Pettis said to fellow candidates that he hoped to come in at least fourth place. His seventh place finish earned him 193 votes, according to county courthouse records.

The 1970 political campaign was the only run for public office Pettis ever made. Ten percent of the candidates running in Hot Springs that year were African American—Pettis was proud to be one of them.

To say that Pettis had an effect on the economy would be putting it mildly. His mother brought him from Mississippi to Hot Springs when he was 7 years old. According to his daughter, Gail, Pettis owned and operated as many as five businesses. In fact, he was the second of three generations in his family to operate a business in Hot Springs: his mother and later his daughter operated local businesses in the city.

The Bulldogs Inn, named after the Langston Bulldog mascot and located near the school, was one of them. He also owned the Starlite Diner on Malvern Avenue and a steakhouse on Central Avenue. These businesses catered to the general public and were classic examples of the need to invest in Hot Springs. Dozens of black-owned businesses existed in Hot Springs in 1970.

Pettis, a savvy businessman who recognized an opportunity when he saw one, used his candidacy to create a boom for his professional career when he ran for mayor. The positive press was good for his thriving businesses.

# Alroy Puckett

Born during the Roaring Twenties, Alroy Puckett would become a man with immeasurable clout in his community.

**Alroy Puckett**

In 1973, Governor Dale Bumpers appointed him as an original member of the Garland County Community College Board of Trustees, according to *The Sentinel-Record*. Puckett served two terms with Mattie L. Collier, the other black appointee and original board member. His second term was unopposed, and it expired on December 31, 1982.

There is a story often retold about how retired Arkansas State Senator Eugene "Bud" Canada recommended Puckett to become a trustee on the original board for what is now the National Park College. Puckett had been previously contacted by Canada to serve in the voluntary position. When Canada asked him a second time to serve, Puckett replied, "Is this another non-paying position?" Indeed it was.

After graduating from Langston High School, he attended trade school in massage therapy in Chicago, Illinois. Upon his return to Hot Springs, he worked as a masseur and as a manager at the National Baptist Hotel and Bathhouse. Becoming hotel manager was only to be

92

expected based on his interpersonal skills with the guests.

When the hotel closed in the 1980s, Puckett noted that it was part of the progress toward achieving integration. To him, the closing was an example of the price of freedom.

Puckett, who had a son to follow him in public office, had a strong relationship with God and the respect of fellow residents. He worked in service of humanity and continued to give of himself as the city continued to grow.

# Garland D. Puckett

When the Hot Springs School District needed diversity, Garland Puckett became the ideal candidate. His only effort for a political office was Position 1 in the 1975 local school board election. Puckett won the election with 564 votes, according to county courthouse records.

The surname Puckett signified a certain pedigree in the community. Garland believed in serving the community just like his father Alroy Puckett. Both were businessmen in addition to being active civic leaders. They hailed from a family of movers and shakers. Records kept at the Visitor's Chapel A.M.E. Church in

On Tuesday, March 11, 1975

Please Vote For

## Garland D. Puckett

### For Position No. 1
ON THE

## HOT SPRINGS SCHOOL BOARD

"Remember . . . He's Number 1 On The Ballot"

**Garland Puckett campaign flyer**

Hot Springs revealed that Garland's great-great-grandfather was a minister of the gospel and a founder of the congregation after the Civil War.

A graduate of Lincoln University in Jefferson City, Missouri, Puckett was one of the founders of CLOB. In those days, Puckett was known for his audacity to expose blatant racism, and he was constantly calling out injustice whenever he witnessed it. Before his career in politics, a young Puckett could be found participating in acts of civil disobedience around the city.

Puckett's election to the school board was during the time of decreased enrollment in the district due to white flight. To assure equal representation of all students, civil rights groups advocated for the elections of school board members by wards. This method had its advantages and disadvantages; however, the election of school board members by wards never happened.

Eventually, Puckett found a career promotion in Pine Bluff. Then the regional Social Security office in Monroe, Louisiana, beckoned him, and he worked there until his retirement. After retirement, Puckett moved back to Hot Springs, where he is actively involved in the Webb Community Center. He stays connected to his spiritual and family roots by supporting the historic Visitor's Chapel A.M.E. Church. Puckett and his wife, Clara, parented two daughters, who are now successful professionals.

Garland Puckett and his father, Alroy, are one of the four father-son political duos to file for office in Hot Springs. The others include William Bonner and Herbert Bonner, Juan Rosborough Sr. and Juan Rosborough Jr., and E.S. Stevenson and Junius Stevenson.

# Juan Ross Rosborough Sr.

In the 1970 election year, more than half a dozen residents in the black community ran for public office. Juan Ross Rosborough Sr. was one of them. He first registered to vote in May 1970 and then ran for alderman in the general election of November 1970, according to the records at the county courthouse.

**Juan Ross Rosborough Sr.**

The Rosboroughs were one of four father-son duos in the black community. Rosborough Sr., a Hot Springs native and service worker at a local lodge, was well established in town. His platform included replacing an old dilapidated and dangerous bridge at Maurice and Valley streets. Rosborough graduated from Langston High School and Philander Smith College in Little Rock. Once referring to himself as "a college tramp," Rosborough was a standout on the Arkansas Baptist College Buffaloes football team in Little Rock.

He served in the Korean War as a soldier in the U.S. Army. While in service, he was married to Alberta McNeal, and the couple had three children. Later, he became an assistant football and basketball coach at Langston, where he also taught physical education.

His activities included his membership at the historic Visitor's Chapel A.M.E. Church, where he served on the steward board and the finance committee. Rosborough was a member of the Garland County Sheriff Patrol and was the head bellman at a local motor lodge. When he wanted to get away from the stress of it all, Rosborough enjoyed riding horses.

After the death of his first wife, Rosborough Sr. later married Mozella Richardson, and they were the parents of one daughter. Rosborough has since passed away. Many years after his death, Mozella married Thomas Anderson, who would become the justice of the peace in District 2.

# Juan Ross Rosborough Jr.

As a 1964 graduate of Langston High School, Juan Ross Rosborough Jr. felt committed to serving his community.

In 1976, he filed for justice of the peace and, later that year, as a candidate for the school board. The family name was a familiar one to his constituency. However, Rosborough, unlike his father, spent many years out of state. Rosborough possessed a talent for public office. He had the natural gifts of a public servant and the appropriate characteristics of a winning candidate. When he approached public official Elmer Beard about suggestions for his candidacy, Beard informed him that he needed to have a job, a position, or title. His response was, "I can always use my uncle's business," referring to Page's Funeral Home.

Rosborough's run for justice of the peace resulted in a run-off election. Kenneth Smith defeated Rosborough with 389 votes to 331, according to county courthouse records. In March 1976, Rosborough made an unsuccessful bid for a seat on the Hot Springs School Board of Education.

He was well liked by his supporters; his opponents admired him, too.

# Elbert Shaw

If Elbert Shaw taught the black political community a lesson, it was this: Winning isn't everything. In fact, sometimes just running is enough.

Shaw, like many black men of his era, wanted to work at the prestigious Arlington Hotel in the 1950s and 1960s. Though he landed a gig as a bellman, he saw no future in this career.

The Hot Springs native developed an interest in politics. Elbert Shaw Jr. of Crete, Illinois, said his father's philosophy was to "get your name in public," offer a service, or run for office. The senior Shaw ran in two elections for city councilman in 1964 and 1968.

The first election was for alderman in Ward 5, which was near the mountains in the uptown section of the city. Shaw was one of two African American candidates running that year for city council; the other candidate was Kenneth Adair, who ran in Ward 2. However, he placed third and lost the election, according to the Garland County Clerk's Office: The total vote was Lonnie Freeman, 3,290; Bob Manor, 2,427; and Shaw, 1,803.

Still, Shaw shined in the election. The total number of supporters for his candidacy revealed he could win in his district and he did. His opponents were unable to win in his Ward 5. However, this was a citywide election in the at-large system, so even though Shaw looked strong in his home ward, he couldn't win the election. This was additional confirmation that supported the long-held claim that the system was stacked against black candidates.

Black candidates over the years did have white allies in politics. Some candidates were able to support each other through an **informal ticket,** which was a verbal-handshake agreement to promote the other's candidacy. Shaw supported Bud Canada, a candidate running for sheriff; this allowed Shaw to solicit support from a cross-section of the electorate.

Shaw's second attempt at office was for Ward 2 city councilman; however, the records don't show his name in the hand-written final tally of the November 5, 1968 election. Shaw Jr. said there was a reason for that: His father dropped out of the race because he felt that the system was designed to prevent him from winning based on the at-large method of voting.

During the election, Shaw Sr. threw his support to a white candidate R.C. "Pook" Parker, who placed fourth out of four candidates, losing the election.

During those days, the likelihood of winning did little to deter candidates like Shaw from running. To him, the numbers didn't matter. "My father always felt like a winner," Shaw Jr. said. Running for public office was a win-win outcome. Even if you lost the race, you won a great deal of positive publicity.

Just filing and getting your name on the ballot after 1954 was the goal of many black residents of Hot Springs and Garland County. Shaw, like many candidates who ran in the 1960s, was mindful of Fred W. Martin, who represented the model for a new age of politics where black people could become more and more involved in all levels of government.

Shaw attended Haven United Methodist Church. His story was like the dozens of *Challengers* who wanted to bring about positive change.

# Todd Simpson

In 1982, Todd Simpson ran for a position on the Garland County Community College Board of Trustees. Kenneth Adair encouraged Simpson's run. Simpson finished fourth out of four candidates but collected an impressive 4,184 votes, according to county courthouse records.

The Rev. Simpson worked in the bathing industry of Bathhouse Row in Hot Springs. When the bathing business declined, he went to work for the Community Service Organization of Garland County, said Leon Massey, the CSO executive director. Simpson started as a custodian and advanced to an outreach worker. Simpson would later become a director of an outreach center.

**Todd Simpson**

An ordained minister at the Union Baptist Church, the Rev. Simpson was able to keep the male chorus organized and disciplined, then-pianist Helen Taylor recalled years later.

One member of the male chorus included Simpson's friend, the late C.P. Warford. Simpson was to give the eulogy at Warford's service, but he lost his speech and notes an hour before the funeral service. However, he recovered nicely. He told Elmer Beard the eulogy was the best sermon he ever preached.

# Charles Wagner Smith

Charles Wagner Smith returned to Hot Springs 25 years ago to embark on a retirement as interesting as his career.

**Charles Wagner Smith**

In 1995, Smith ran for Arkansas State Representative, receiving 31 percent of the vote but didn't win the election, according to records at the county courthouse. In 2000, Smith ran for Hot Springs mayor. He didn't win the election, but he received a solid 30 percent of the vote.

A native of Hot Springs, Smith served in the U.S. Army during the Vietnam era. He completed courses in labor relations at the University of Illinois and secured teaching credentials from the State of California. Later, he became an operation officer, training coordinator, and branch manager in Watts and Southern California. After 30 years of service in Social Security, he retired in 1990, and returned to Hot Springs, where he founded his company, CWS Associates. His company served the Department of Human Services in Garland and Montgomery counties.

In that capacity, he served as a community development specialist coordinating programs and services. As a member of the NAACP, he has addressed and served as master of ceremonies for many programs since he returned to Hot Springs. In the 1990s, he was the executive director and chairman of the board of the Webb Community Center.

Programs there were developed with structure and provided the center with the kind of organization that it had never had. Smith's training and consultant preparations and experience have provided services for residents in Mississippi, Louisiana, and Arkansas.

Also, as an accomplished playwright, Smith's works have been performed on stages across the country in Chicago, Illinois; Milwaukee, Wisconsin; and the Wilshire Ebell Theater in Los Angeles, California. With his excellent communication skills, he hosted and promoted a weekly television talk show, *Everyday People*, on Resort Cable Television in Hot Springs.

A motivational speaker, he is the founder of the thespian group Prolific Arts Performers and Stepping Stones in Chicago and Los Angeles. He served on the Arkansas Rehabilitation Advisory Council, 1993–1995. In May 1997, he was appointed to the State Board of Workforce Education. In addition to his public speaking and monologues at luncheons, banquets, and other occasions, Smith provides grant training for agencies each year for the United Way of Garland County. He and his late wife, Geri, are of the Catholic faith. They are the parents of two sons, U.S. Reed and Stephen Patoc.

When asked in an interview why he ran for public office, he quipped, "It's better to be a part of the community than apart from it."

---

## DID YOU KNOW?

Charles Smith worked in casting for Alex Haley's ABC miniseries, *Roots*, filling in as an extra.

---

# Kenneth Smith

Kenneth Smith was a three-time political candidate in Hot Springs. While all of his candidacies were not documented with the Garland County Elections Commission, this is an official attempt to set the record straight.

**Kenneth Smith**

Smith ran for city councilman, school board member, and justice of the peace. Smith remembers each of these campaigns as does one-time opponent Elmer Beard. During that time, however, the Garland County Election Commission only maintained records for political candidates who won their races and not the runners-up.

There were remnants of his 1974 bid for alderman. His campaign cards indicated he was "A Friend of the Community—Vote for Ken Smith, Your Friend." Smith advocated that the alderman stipend be used to rent office space for Ward 3 so residents could have a place to voice concerns they had in the community. This proposal never materialized. Smith was defeated in his run for city council by the incumbent Alderman Beard.

It is also known, that Smith ran for the school board in 1975 and lost the election although he received more than 1,000 votes. However, the written record that has been preserved on microfilm at *The Sentinel-Record* reveals nothing about his participation in this race.

This lack of record-keeping may affect future biographies of local residents. For example, Smith was elected as a Garland County Quorum Court Justice of the Peace in 1976. He represented District 9 in the then-recently revised county districts. This time there was a record of his candidacy in a Garland County Election Commission report because he was the winner but no mentions of his opponents. In recent years, the county election commission has included the information on all candidates running for public office.

Prior to Smith's political career, he attended Wilson City College and King College in Chicago, Illinois. He served his country during the Vietnam War from 1962–1966 in the U.S. Air Force. After his discharge from the military, Smith returned to Hot Springs, where he became active in the community and served as a deacon at the Ebenezer Baptist Church.

Smith served as justice of the peace until his resignation in November 1977, when he moved to Little Rock. During the last quarter of a century, Smith was as community-minded as they came. He was a NAACP state vice president for 14 years, president of the Webb Community Center Board of Directors, and a director of the annual Dr. Martin Luther King Jr. Parade.

"Politics has always been in our family," Smith said. He and his brother, Charles Smith, are one of only two sets of brothers who ran for public office in Hot Springs. They hailed from Tweedle Town, one of the first black communities in the Spa City. Tweedle Town dated back four generations, and the Smiths are also descendants of the Tweedle family.

# Rev. Michael Smith

The Rev. Michael Smith is a businessman and pastor of New Beginning Ministries on East Grand Avenue in Hot Springs.

Smith filed for the city Board of Directors District 2. He was defeated by Elaine Jones by 21 votes in the 2007 election, according to the Garland County Clerk's Office. After the election, Smith asked for a recount. The practice of a recount comes at the expense of the defeated candidate. No recount occurred.

Smith, a Pine Bluff native, is known for his friendliness and hopefulness. Since he has lived in Hot Springs, he has been a man of influence in many areas of the community.

**Rev. Michael and Sarah Smith**

The Rev. Smith ran a campaign calling for a change. In a recent interview, he repeatedly pleaded for more visibility in his neighborhood: improved street maintenance, increased police patrol, and the presence of a director representing District 2.

Smith also manages Sarah's Precious Day Care Center on Illinois Street. Smith's child-care center is named in honor of Sarah, his wife. The business is in the shadow of what residents once called the **Black Projects**, across the street from the Wade Street Park. The City of Hot Springs was applauded for its efforts to re-name the street after the daycare center.

With a continued interest in District 2, Smith's business day begins with his non-denominational congregation and the family daycare business. Bubbling with pride, Smith said Sarah's Precious Day Care, as of 2010, was the only African American operated daycare in Hot Springs. Sarah's Precious Day Care is in part sponsored by the NAACP Unit 6013, which supports the daycare's Back to School Backpack Program.

Smith always strives for improvements in District 2. One example Smith has followed has been to encourage people to register to vote and to join the NAACP. Residents can sign up for either of these opportunities at the Webb Community Center or at Sarah's Precious Day Care.

# E. S. Stevenson

Having moved to Hot Springs from Dallas County, E.S. Stevenson spent most of his life in service work and hotel management. In 1968, he filed to run as city alderman. This was during the at-large election system of voting. Stevenson's bid was unsuccessful, according to county courthouse records.

Stevenson was a member of the historic Roanoke Baptist Church, where he served as a deacon for 40 years. After the church was destroyed by fire in 1963, at the height of the civil rights struggle, he joined the Greater St. Paul Baptist Church.

Many of the black candidates won only in their wards and Stevenson complained that the system was unfair and should be changed. Every black candidate proved that the odds in at-large voting were stacked against them.

The NAACP and other civic organizations consumed the time and interest of Stevenson and other candidates who paved the way for a new generation of leaders. These leaders saluted him and others for their pioneering and trailblazing spirit. According to the NAACP's record, E.S. Stevenson and later his son, Junius, were one of four father-son duos to run for public office in the black community.

# Junius Stevenson

Junius Stevenson, son of *Challenger* E.S. Stevenson, was a candidate for justice of the peace and the Hot Springs Board of Directors. He was unsuccessful in both attempts.

The native of Sparkman moved with his parents to Hot Springs when he was 3 years old. Stevenson was reared in Hot Springs and attended separate and unequal schools.

Gifted in music, Stevenson was trained in a band

**From left: Marcus Phillips, Stevenson, and Ana Getzoff**

sponsored by philanthropist John L. Webb. This band rehearsed in the basement of the historic Roanoke Baptist Church, where Stevenson was taught music.

Music was his avocation, but science was his vocation and major at Tennessee State University in Nashville. After graduation, Stevenson moved to Chicago, Illinois. While working for the U.S. Postal Service, he earned his master's degree in education and taught in the Chicago school system.

Upon retiring, this conservative educator returned to his family roots, his father's estate, and Roanoke. He got involved with the NAACP, **Recognizing Everyone's Gifts And Respecting Diversity** (REGARD), the Central Democratic Committee, and the Hot Springs Planning Commission. He and his wife, Peggy, sponsored the *Ebony* Fashion Show for many years.

He spent so many hours volunteering at the Webb Community Center that many thought he was a salaried employee, which he wasn't. While gaining experience into the public sector, he considered running for public office.

In 1994, as a candidate for city director in District 1, he received 30 percent of the vote. In his race for Justice of the Peace District 1, the results were 727 for Alan Clark to 573 for Stevenson, according to county courthouse records. Although he did not win the elections, he was proud of the number of votes he received.

Residents continue to speak fondly of the mild-mannered son who followed in his father's footsteps. Stevenson died December 31, 2006.

# Isaac Thomas

In 1970, Isaac Thomas ran for mayor of Hot Springs. Thomas finished in eighth place of the 11 candidates for mayor, according to the Garland County Clerk's Office. Election results gave him 137 votes and 3,938 votes to the winner, Tom Ellsworth.

Thomas was a native of Newellton, Louisiana. Like most of Thomas' generation, he was the first in his family to run for public office.

This striking man was the doting father with his wife, Antee, of five sons and five daughters. Much of his career was spent as a spa attendant at the bathhouses in Hot Springs. He was known for his family photo that he kept posted for all his clients to see and admire. After pointing out his family portrait, Thomas would often persuade his clients to tip well by saying, "If you could find it in your

**Thomas, holding Connie, with wife, Antee; from left: Bernadean, Amanda, Velma, Danny, Veter, Vercy, Isaac, Johnny, and Wilbert**

heart to give anything extra ... I have 10 mouths to feed."

While Thomas was running for mayor, his daughter Velma used her charm and beauty to break down a racial barrier of her own in Hot Springs. It started when the Council of the Liberation of Blacks (CLOB) demonstrated on the last night of the 1969 Miss Arkansas Pageant, which was held annually in the city. John Paschal, president of CLOB, declared, "Don't bring your lily-white pageant back here unless you have a black contestant."

Velma Thomas: *The Sentinel-Record*

That next year, Velma, who sang the love theme from *Romeo and Juliet* in alto, became the first African American woman to be crowned Miss Hot Springs. She went on to compete in the Miss Arkansas Pageant in 1970. She lost the title, but her presence, alone, was a win for her people.

Once named "Parents of the Year" with his wife, Thomas was a father proud of each of his children. His son Isaac Thomas Jr., a star quarterback at Langston High School, would go on to play football for the Dallas Cowboys.

Thomas attended the historic Roanoke Baptist Church, where he served on the deacon board and sang in the male chorus. He was well known for taking his children to Sunday School and church every week. Some of his children attended Roanoke as adults and brought their children, continuing the tradition.

# Raymond "Honey" Tweedle

Raymond "Honey" Tweedle, who grew up in a family that took politics seriously, ran twice for the Hot Springs City Council. He was a member of one of the oldest black families in the city, but his popularity would offer him few advantages in the campaign.

**Raymond "Honey" Tweedle**

Despite the slim chance, the businessman would test out the racial climate after *Brown v. Board of Education of Topeka, Kansas*, with a run for public office in 1954. Fred Martin and Tweedle were the only black candidates to run in Hot Springs that year; both ran for the position of alderman at a time when voting rights were not even secured for many African Americans in the South.

Tweedle's bid was unsuccessful, while Martin's was a triumph because of the Martin Mix-up. Tweedle's second bid in 1956 was also unsuccessful, according to records at the county courthouse. However, each effort was a boost to voter registration and the various personal businesses he operated on the famed Malvern Avenue.

He operated a newsstand in the black-owned Pythian Hotel. The newsstand became a popular gathering place for many residents who wanted to catch the latest on politics in the community. On occasion, news reporters would stop by for news tips.

Born on August 17, 1914, Tweedle received a public education in the Hot Springs segregated school system. He was married to Gladys Banks of Beloit, Wisconsin, and they raised four children. Throughout his life, he attended Ebenezer Baptist Church, St. Paul A.M.E. Church, and Haven United Methodist Church.

Perhaps most notably, he is part of the famed Tweedle family of which the neighborhood, Tweedle Town, around Jones school is named. One of the living descendants, Charles Smith, described the community in an issue of *The Kettle*, the publication of the Melting Pot Genealogical Society of Hot Springs, Fall 2010: "Our neighborhood was comprised of a mix of black families and white families," Smith relayed in the article, adding, "many of which were Tweedles or Tweedle-related."

Raymond Tweedle and Fred W. Martin were pioneers in their campaigns for public office in the black community during the Jim Crow era. Prior to 1954, if Tweedle and Freddie Martin had filed for public office, it would have been dangerous.

To have blacks running for office was beyond the imagination of the African American community. This was a powerful stand on the part of Tweedle and Martin. They were the first two *Challengers*.

---

## DID YOU KNOW?

Tweedle Town was bound by West Grand Avenue on the north side, Summer Street on the east side, Albert Pike on the south side, and a wooded area to the west side.

---

# Debbie Ugbade

To run for a position and win the race the first time is rare, but Debbie Ugbade accomplished this feat in 2000 and every election thereafter.

Her success at the polling places says a lot about Ugbade, who is community-minded.

Ugbade has brought a sense of professionalism to her Hot Springs school board position. The NAACP Unit 6013 applauded Ugbade's career and service to her community because she has been one of the group's most active members. She is also involved in the Airport Road Church of Christ and has served on the Webb Community Center Board of Directors.

**Debbie Ugbade**

Ugbade was as a public affairs specialist with the Ouachita National Forest Service. She is a native of Paris, Arkansas, and received a bachelor's degree in psychology from Arkansas Tech in Russellville. Later, she earned a master's degree in adult education from the University of Arkansas in Fayetteville.

Ugbade and her husband, Festus, are the parents of three grown children. All of them attended public schools in Hot Springs. "I've enjoyed being on the school board," Ugbade said when she worked with Joyce Craft. "We are a team with the superintendent. We strive for the same goals not only to help the students but also to help make Hot Springs the best school district it can be."

# George Watson

George Watson ran twice for Hot Springs City Council in Ward 1. In 1972, he lost to Les Ashley by a vote of 863–94, according to county courthouse records. In 1974, he lost to Lloyd Wacaster by a vote of 462–61.

George Watson

Living in Hot Springs in 1984, he criticized the alderman from his district. Watson complained about how the lack of presence in the black community showed a lack of concern for a segment of the voters. "I don't see you until the election and then you come sticking your hand out," Watson once declared publicly.

In 1985, as a result of his political activism, the city council appointed Watson to the Civil Service Commission. While serving on the commission, he was instrumental in the employment of firefighter Paul Green to the Hot Springs Fire Department. Police Officer William Watkins also was promoted during Watson's tenure.

A native of Texarkana, Texas, he was a counselor at Ouachita Job Corps. He also became Humphrey's Dairy's first black milkman. Buying white milk from a black man brought a chuckle to many Humphrey's Dairy's customers.

During his stint at the Reynolds Metal Company, Watson relocated to Portland, Oregon, in 1987. He died there on January 1, 2013, leaving behind his wife, Betty Jo, and their family to carry on his legacy.

# Harriel Dean White

Harriel White bested his opponent, Tim B. Sassaman Jr., in the September 1988 Hot Springs School Board election. White received about 62 percent of the votes to Sassaman's 37 percent, according to school district records.

To prepare for public service, White graduated from Langston High School. He served in Vietnam, and after being honorably discharged, he returned home to earn a bachelor's degree from Henderson State University in Arkadelphia. Although he was qualified to teach junior high science, having done his student teaching at Hot Springs High School, he only taught for a short while.

When he wasn't in the classroom, the Rev. White was in the pulpit, serving as pastor of the St. Paul A.M.E. Church in Hot Springs and other congregations around the state. At home, he was husband to Shirlene Puckett and the father to two sons.

White's term on the school board was interrupted with his resignation. His Social Security Administration work relocated him at different times in his career. When White returned to Hot Springs, there was a vacancy on the school board. Then-Superintendent Roy Rowe mentioned White's name for the position. Without opposition, White was appointed to complete an unexpired term as of September 20, 1995, according to the school board minutes. After this appointment, White never filed for election again.

In 1996, White expressed reservations to community activist Elmer Beard regarding the employment of one school administrator who would be the new principal at Hot Springs High School. White was concerned that the administrator had too little experience in working with a diverse student body that was represented at the high school. The school board hired the administrator but it was without White's vote. In the end, the school board and White were pleased with the job of the principal, still White never regretted his dissenting vote.

After he left the school board, White remained involved in the issues affecting his former constituents. In 1998, the school district records contained a case of an African American female employee who had to appear before the school board over claims of insubordination. At her hearing, White who was an officer of the local NAACP at the time, defended her actions and garnered the support of more than 30 residents to rally behind her at a school board meeting. The meeting which, was more than three hours long, resulted in the employee being released from the Hot Springs school system and hired in a different school district. His defense was noteworthy.

**Officers of the NAACP Unit 6013 in 2002; from left: Elmer Beard, Faye Hildreth, Kelsey King, and Harriel White**

# Birkes Williams

Birkes Williams was a two-time candidate and declared winner for the Hot Springs School Board Position 2.

**Birkes Williams**

In September 1996, Williams won almost 64 percent of the vote against Rick Stuart and Tim Hutson, according to the Garland County Court House records. There was large voter turnout because of a tax increase on the ballot, which passed by a vote of 246–157.

In September 1999, Williams was re-elected to his second three-year term. However, he resigned before his term expired, due to a possible professional conflict of interest with the school board.

He championed for a diverse staff in the schools to positively influence the diverse student body. "I was concerned about the configuration of students with faculty and staff who looked like us," Williams said. "There was not enough effort being made to recruit African Americans."

Williams encouraged a strong relationship between the teachers and students. "They weren't reaching out to African American students to help them acquire the skills they would need to be successful," he said. He believed a coach ought to be able to identify with his players on and off the field. A good coach should be concerned with a player's home life, his living conditions, and his after-school activities, Williams said.

He strongly supported Coach Alfred Mohammed being named to the head football position at Hot Springs High School. To this day, Williams considers it an accomplishment that he had played a role in hiring the first African American to fill that position. "Coach Mohammed had connections with universities and recruiters and did more to get his athletes scholarships than any other coach had done," Williams said.

His overall service on the board increased the respect the administration had for the worth of black educators and administrators, according to public comments made at a luncheon in his honor.

Two gubernatorial administrations appointed Williams to serve on committees. The first was former Governor Bill Clinton who appointed Williams for one term on the Human Services Reorganization Committee and the Social Work Licensing Board. When former Governor Jim Guy Tucker succeeded Clinton, Williams continued serving on the Licensing Board as vice chairman.

Williams and his wife, Brenda, were graduates of the University of Arkansas in Pine Bluff. He also graduated from the University of Arkansas in Little Rock with a master's degree and was a licensed clinical social worker. His wife is a teacher at Hot Springs High School. Their two children, both having graduated from the Hot Springs School District, went on to have prestigious careers in the armed forces.

The Williams family's church is the historic Roanoke Baptist Church in Hot Springs of which the former school board member serves as a deacon.

# Rev. Willie Davis Young

In 1976, the Rev. Willie Davis Young ran for Hot Springs City Councilman for Ward 3. He lost the election, according to November 1976 records at the Garland County Clerk's Office.

**Rev. Willie Davis Young**

A Rosston native, the Rev. Young was licensed to preach at Eureka Baptist Church in Hot Springs. Outside of the pulpit and political ring, he may have been best known in the Spa City as a concrete finisher.

Though he was unsuccessful at the ballot box, running for office allowed the Rev. Young to make worthwhile business connections. Ten years after his campaign, he would receive a government assignment that would make him beam with joy. The Rev. Young was hired to do a concrete job on the grounds of the State Capitol Building in Little Rock. His wife, Floralene, remembers how proud he was of the $5,300 job and the honor of working with the Secretary of State's Office. His wife said the contracting work was part of a family business; the couple had six children, including five sons.

The Korean War veteran served his country and was honorably discharged. The Rev. Young was always a soldier on another battlefield, establishing a rich record in the church community in Hot Springs. He joined St. Mark's Baptist Church on Crescent Street, which was his church home until his death in 1987.

# GLOSSARY

## African Methodist Episcopal

Established in 1816, the African Methodist Episcopal (A.M.E.) Church began in Philadelphia. Its founder, former-slave-turned-abolitionist Richard Allen, protested the racial discrimination he and fellow clergyman Absolom Jones suffered in the white congregation at St. George's Methodist Episcopal Church.

In 1787, Allen and Jones left the church and formed the Quaker-influenced Free African Society, where they were able to preach their values. Allen founded Bethel A.M.E. Church in 1794, a stop on the Underground Railroad.

According to church history, Allen successfully sued in Pennsylvania courts for the right of his congregation to exist as an independent institution. Bethel A.M.E. Church, 22 years later, would spawn an entire denomination known simply as African Methodist Episcopal. With 19 Episcopal districts and 2.5 million members, the A.M.E. is the largest black Methodist denomination in the nation.

Allen's church in Philadelphia, renamed Mother Bethel A.M.E., is a national historic landmark and remains the oldest property continuously owned by African Americans.

## African Methodist Episcopal Zion

African Methodist Episcopal Zion was founded by James Varick in 1821 in New York City. Varick, the son of slaves, left the John Street Methodist Church over segregation in the worship services and in the burial grounds.

In 1796, Varick and other members formed the African Methodist Episcopal Zion Church, according to church history. Slavery was still practiced in New York so some members were enslaved and freed Africans.

There are many similarities between the first A.M.E. denomination and the A.M.E. Zion denomination that was organized five years later. Both were established by abolitionists because of racially restrictive policies in the Methodist Episcopal Church. Initially both denominations were called African Methodist Episcopal, until 1848 when Zion was added to recognize the name of its first church and distinguish it from the Philadelphia denomination.

Abolitionists Frederick Douglass, Sojourner Truth, and Harriet Tubman were members of the A.M.E. Zion Church.

## At-Large Voting

At-large voting is the mass voting that was under the mayor-alderman form of government in Hot Springs from 1921–1970. Every voter could select up to two candidates from any ward, regardless of residency. This allowed voters to elect political candidates to represent districts where the candidate may or may not have resided. This system made it nearly impossible for black candidates to be elected, whereas election-by-district proved to be a more equitable approach.

## Black and White Projects

Known as the Black Projects, these multi-unit apartment buildings were part of the Hot Springs Housing Authority. They were built to segregate residents in the early 1960s and provide a rent-regulated, higher standard of living for low-income residents. The Black Projects are around Silver and Illinois streets, east of East Grand Avenue. The White Projects are on the southwest side of East Grand and Convention Boulevard and the Spring Street area.

The Housing Authority, once an all-white board, was desegregated in the 1970s, only after the NAACP, CLOB, and others petitioned the board to "do what was right."

## Christian Methodist Episcopal

Initially, C.M.E. was an abbreviation for Colored Methodist Episcopal, a primarily black denomination originating in 1870 in Jackson, Tennessee. In 1954, the name changed to Christian Methodist Episcopal.

According to church history, it was founded by 41 former slaves from the Methodist Episcopal Church to promote the interest of its colored members. It has nine Episcopal districts across the nation and two on the African continent; the church is headquartered in Memphis, Tennessee.

## Council of the Liberation of Blacks

In 1969, a civil rights group formed in a local bar on the famed black business district along Malvern Avenue. The bar attracted a younger, more radical set who differed from the old guard of the NAACP and church community. The Council of the Liberation of Blacks (CLOB) fought for economic equality and social justice. Ringleader John Paschal and members Edward Martin, Garland Puckett, Eddie Scott, and Elmer Beard were known as agitators. They would often participate at the Hot Springs

John Paschal of CLOB

City Council meetings. The group focused on issues such as diversifying the workforce, desegregating local stores, integrating public education, and redistricting the wards.

One of the first demonstrations was demanding a black contestant at the all-white Miss Arkansas pageant since the event came to the Spa City each year. Also during that time, the all-black Langston High School was in the process of integrating with the mostly white Hot Springs High School. It was not a smooth transition, and CLOB protested with students to ensure their voices were heard.

After a couple of years, CLOB dissolved when some members left town and other members began working inside the system to achieve the goals of the council.

## Drafted

Many candidates are drafted for office. This means that they are selected by an individual or group to run. Sometimes candidates have people promoting their campaign before the person has made a public announcement committing to run. When no one takes the lead to run for office, it may become necessary to draft.

On at least two occasions, Raymond Tart and Bob Hansen, both members of the Central Democratic Committee, encouraged or drafted an African American to file for public office like *Challenger* Aaron Gordon.

## Election Commission

The election commission was used to set the rules for running elections and ensuring an accurate vote count of the ballots. Each county in Arkansas had a three-member commission: Two members represented the majority party and one member represented the minority party. The arrangement allowed the majority party to wield great influence on the local electoral system because the commission was responsible for all the details of the election. The Democratic and Republican parties determined who would be its commission representatives.

## First Lady

Normally and formally used to describe the wife of the President of the United States, first lady is a term used very casually in the black community and in modern English. Often churches will refer to the wife of the pastor of a church as its first lady. It can also be used in other connotations referring to the wife of a man in leadership.

## Form of Government

Since the 20$^{th}$ Century, Hot Springs has had two major forms of government—mayor-alderman and manager-board. Under the mayor-alderman, which was in use until 1986, the government was run by the mayor working with a city council. Under the manager-board, which is still in use today, the government is run by a city manager working with a board of directors; the mayor and board of directors hire the city manager.

The major difference: under the old system, all positions were salaried; under the new system only the city manager is salaried. Also, the city directors have staggered terms. From 1970–1986, it was possible that all city council members could be new at the same time with no experience or continuity of leadership. That situation couldn't happen with the manager-board form of government.

## Garland County Re-Apportionment Commission

During the 1960s, the electoral process in Hot Springs came under fire. In 1969, Mayor Dan Wolf took a stand and urged the city aldermen to approve a re-apportionment commission to evaluate how voters elected public officials to represent them. City Attorney Curtis Ridgway counseled the mayor and the aldermen, who then approved the appointment of one African American and a representative from both political parties to the three-member Garland County Re-Apportionment Commission. The members were Elmer Beard, Dan McGraw, and Robert Corrodo. Then-attorney Henry Britt, who would later become circuit judge, was appointed to be the advisor to direct the bipartisan commission.

**Attorney Curtis Ridgway**

**Judge Henry Britt**

Britt photo: The Sentinel-Record

Beard (right), Adair, Justice of the Peace Wendall Hilton and Logan listen to commission members.
(Photo by David Glenn)

# Ward redistricting remains in discussion

**The Sentinel-Record covered city officials mulling over redistricting.**

By March of 1970, the commission had done what it was assigned to do. It re-apportioned the city's eight wards into six wards. It also voted to have aldermen elected to office only representing the ward in which they lived, according to the August 1969 city council guidelines. The results of the commission were meant to influence any future re-districting of wards, based on U.S. Census reports, so that the work to give people of color a voice wasn't undermined.

The success of the commission hinged on the support of the city council, Hot Springs Chamber of Commerce, CLOB, and the NAACP Unit 6013.

## Gerrymandering

Gerrymandering is the practice of creating political districts in weird shapes to preserve a voting majority for the governing leader of the time. Its origin dates back to 1812 when Governor Elbridge Gerry of Massachusetts drew the lines of one district in his state. Pundits said it looked like the shape of a salamander.

A newspaper played on the word and reported that the lines were a "Gerrymander." Governor Gerry lost the following election but the district remained a stronghold of members of his party. The name gerrymander became part of the American political system.

## Honoraria

Prior to 1986, city aldermen had been paid. Justices of the Peace were paid honoraria for attending meetings. An honorarium is a reward for services that customs or propriety forbids a price to be set. Sometimes, for travel or a speaking engagement, an honorarium is presented to a person as a courtesy. In more recent years in Hot Springs, city directors have served without pay. College and school board members also have served without pay.

## Informal Ticket

Candidates ran for office on the same informal ticket, which was a verbal contract between two candidates. Both agree to support each other in their individual campaigns for office. A candidate would say—pardon the pronoun manners—"vote for me and John." In more modern times, a black candidate would run with a white candidate, but this practice was unheard of before 1954.

## Jim Crow

Jim Crow laws were state-sanctioned oppression that restricted the civil rights and liberties of black citizens. African Americans had limited access to education, housing, transportation, commerce, healthcare, and public facilities. These state and municipal laws were upheld by a separate-but-equal doctrine based on the U.S. Supreme Court decision in *Plessy v. Ferguson* (1896). The system was partly dismantled by federal legislation and Supreme Court rulings in the 1950s and 1960s.

However, after landmark court decisions, discrimination continues. The 13th Amendment abolished slavery, but an exception allows the system to operate in the modern era: "Neither slavery nor involuntary servitude, except as a punishment for crime whereof the party shall have been duly convicted, shall exist within the United States ..."

This loophole is constitutional justification for slavery to flourish in today's society. Statistics show that there are more blacks imprisoned in the United States today than at the height of apartheid in South Africa. In fact, there are more African Americans under correctional control than were enslaved in 1850, according to the 2010 book *The New Jim Crow: Mass Incarceration in the Age of Colorblindness* by Michelle Alexander. "It's perfectly legal to discriminate against people with criminal histories in nearly all the ways that it was once legal to discriminate against African Americans," Alexander wrote.

"Once you're labeled a felon, the old forms of discrimination—employment discrimination, housing discrimination, denial of the right to vote, denial of educational opportunity, denial of food stamps and other public benefits, and exclusion from jury service—are suddenly legal. As a convicted felon, you have scarcely more rights, and arguably less respect, than a black man living in Alabama at the height of Jim Crow. We have not ended racial caste in America; we have merely redesigned it."

## The Martin Mix-Up

In 1954, an black man named Fred Martin was elected to the Hot Springs City Council. It was an unbelievable feat for residents to put a black man in office during Jim Crow. In fact, many white residents who voted for Martin felt they made a mistake. They assumed they were voting for Clifford Martin, a white businessman who was widely known in political ranks in Hot Springs. The morning after the historic election, many voters stormed the Garland County Court House demanding that their vote be changed. There was nothing that could be done at that point. The vote count stood, and Fred Martin became the first black man elected to public office in the modern era.

**The white candidate Clifford Martin in 1954 campaign card**

☆ Your Vote Is Your Personal Privilege. May I Have Yours? ☆

## CLIFFORD MARTIN

Candidate For

## Alderman 7th Ward

2

General Election, Nov. 2, 1954

# NAACP

The National Association for the Advancement of Colored People (NAACP) is the largest and oldest civil rights organization in the country. It was founded in 1909 by a group of black and white liberals and most notably Harvard-educated scholar and Pan-Africanist W.E.B. DuBois. The organization, specifically its Legal Defense Fund, may be credited with many of the gains African Americans have made in this country since Reconstruction.

Harvard-educated lawyer Charles Hamilton Houston, who served as the NAACP's first special counsel, is recognized as the man who killed Jim Crow laws. In the 1930s, Houston would lay the groundwork for the legal defense team to fight for anti-lynching legislation, school desegregation, fair housing, and voting rights.

Houston protégé Thurgood Marshall would lead the NAACP's Legal Defense Fund, successfully arguing *Brown v. Board of Education* before the U.S. Supreme Court. The case reversed the decades-old separate-but-equal doctrine of *Plessy v. Ferguson* (1896). The landmark decision federally mandated an end to segregated schools and later secured Marshall a seat on the nation's highest bench, making him the first African American U.S. Supreme Court Justice.

When a young seamstress Rosa Parks refused to give up her seat on a bus, it was the NAACP that organized the 381-day Bus Boycott in Montgomery, Alabama. That successful protest, which desegregated the public transit system in Alabama, launched the career of a young minister named the Rev. Dr. Martin Luther King Jr.

## NAACP Unit 6013

Today, the NAACP Unit 6013, like hundreds of chapters across the nation, continues the struggle for equality on a local level. Formally created on November 11, 1942, the chapter was designed to eliminate segregation in education, employment, politics, and the community. The organizers were men, but there was a lot of support from women and white people.

The chapter was secretly chartered during discussions in city hotel linen closets and homes on Malvern and Central avenues in Hot Springs. It was often said that members kept their membership cards hidden inside their shoes.

## One Man, One-Vote System

The one-man, one-vote (one-person, one-vote) system resulted from redistricting efforts of the Garland County Re-Apportionment Commission from 1969–1970. The system required candidates to represent only the district in which the candidates lived. Voters and candidates from diverse communities found this system more engaging.

## Poll Tax

One of the many tactics used to disenfranchise black voters in the South was the poll tax. In Arkansas before the mid-1960s, as elsewhere in the South, a poll tax was a fixed amount of money that a voter had to pay before he or she could vote. The poll tax was paid to the county clerk. Voters could walk into the courthouse and pay the poll tax at any point in time up to 30 days before the election.

Voters then received a receipt showing they paid the poll tax. This receipt would be shown at an election precinct

**Poll Tax Receipt of Rosa Parks from the U.S. Library of Congress**

as proof the person was registered to vote. In turn, the election precinct would give the person a ballot.

In Arkansas, the poll tax amount was $1 per person per year. The rules also allowed a person to pay the poll tax for another individual without the individual being present. This was how some local leaders influenced people to vote for them. The system was so flawed that at times it was possible for a person to pay a poll tax for a deceased resident. This fee was not only a method used to turn black voters away from the polls, it also discouraged poor whites and Native Americans from voting.

## REGARD

REGARD was formed in 2001 in Hot Springs. The name is an acronym for Recognizing Everyone's Gifts and Respecting Diversity. Behind the letters is a nonprofit organization made up of culturally, racially, and religiously diverse members. The community-oriented group meets regularly and works with the schools and the Garland County Library organizing programs that promote peace, tolerance, and understanding.

## Roanoke Baptist Church

Of the 63 *Challengers*, 15 were members of the historic Roanoke Baptist Church, which was founded by freed slaves and their masters in 1868. More than a sanctuary, it was a school and the cornerstone of the black community.

In a rash of arsons that have destroyed black churches since their establishment in America, the church lit up the night sky when it erupted into flames. According to the December 22, 1963, edition of *The Sentinel-Record*, the fire that engulfed the 95-year-old church was labeled as "mysterious." The building, located in the 300 block of Whittington Avenue, was insured for only $33,000.

A major piece of Hot Springs history had been diminished to ashes. Eyewitnesses said they saw smoke from

**The historic Roanoke Baptist Church before the 1963 fire**

133

the fire several miles away and for many hours that Sunday morning. Members, friends, and supporters cried.

For months, the Rev. James Donald Rice had been receiving threatening telephone calls. They were short and to the point, accusing the minister of being an agitator involved with desegregation protests in Hot Springs. At this time, Rev. Rice also was the president of the NAACP Unit 6013.

At about 4:45 A.M. just three days before Christmas 1963, a man assumed to be white,

Rev. James Donald Rice

phoned Rev. Rice. The caller declared, "You have been warned to stop your trouble-making work in the local NAACP. Now look out the door and see what's happening to your church." Rev. Rice remained calm and asked the caller to please repeat what he had said for clarity. Rice then handed the phone to his wife, Ellen, who was also awakened by the pre-dawn call. The caller repeated his exact words to her.

The nearest fire station to the church at that time was on Whittington Avenue near the former St. Joseph's Hospital. An eyewitness revealed that a firefighter with an axe ran from the fire station for about three blocks to the church. After the fire, the firefighter shared privately with Rev. Rice that a back door had been broken open, a pile of cushions from the pews had been piled in the center section of the church, and this stack was the tinder that set the beautiful edifice ablaze.

Years later, the pastor returned for the 135th church anniversary celebration and told his former members that he would never reveal the white firefighter's name to protect his identity and safety. Rev. Rice kept his word as he had promised believing it was the will of God that only the edifice was destroyed and not the spirit of the church body or the faith of its members. One of the first contributors to the rebuilding effort was a local white priest, who wanted to remain anonymous.

Rev. Rice wasn't the only Hot Springs pastor to receive church-burning threats. The Rev. J.J. Brown, pastor of Visitor's Chapel A.M.E., also was warned by Klansmen to disconnect himself from the NAACP. Rev. Brown was the vice president of the local NAACP. Soon after these threats were received, Rev. Brown was transferred to Bethel A.M.E. Church in Malvern.

Both Rev. Rice and Rev. Brown told these same stories for decades. Rice said not one investigator from the state fire marshal, the Hot Springs Fire Chief Vern Smith, Prosecuting Attorney David Whittington, or the FBI ever contacted him. In fact, it wasn't until United Press International contacted *The Sentinel-Record* that the local paper finally contacted Rev. Rice. In February 2003, Rev. Rice returned to Hot Springs and shared details of this historical account in a speech titled, "Memory/History" at the historic Roanoke Baptist Church.

## Spa City

Officially known by its postal name, Hot Springs National Park, the city also is known by its nickname, "The American Spa." According to the National Park Foundation, the area was established as a reservation by the U.S. Congress in 1832, four years before the state of Arkansas was admitted to the union. Billing itself as the nation's "Original National Park" and "America's First Resort," Hot Springs is the oldest protected land in the national park system.

The hot springs, for which the city surrounded by mountains is named, flow from the ground at around 140 degrees Fahrenheit. Hot water is the main source of the city's tourism built on healing thermal baths that were once in the nine federal bathhouses that line the downtown district. In its heyday, Bathhouse Row and hotels attracted an international enclave of guests from Al Capone, Helen Keller, Babe Ruth, and President Theodore Roosevelt. It also drew many African American newcomers and visitors to the city, where they were welcomed to thrive in the bustling economy as long as they stayed in their place.

## Spa Development Corporation

In 1984, the Spa Development Corp. was made up of 10 members organized primarily for saving the National Baptist Hotel and Bathhouse on Malvern Avenue. The intention was to develop the historic building into a casino when gambling became legal in Hot Springs in the mid-1980s. Each member invested $300 in the corporation. Gambling, however, was never legalized. The corporation folded after a couple of years.

## Staggered Terms

This is a system designed to ensure continuity of leadership by alternating terms of board members so all the terms will end at different times. It prevents a board from having inexperienced all-new elected officials or all-new appointed members at the same time.

When the Hot Springs City Council had staggered terms from 1917 to 1970 for the election of aldermen, one alderman per ward was elected in even-numbered years and the other alderman per ward was elected in odd-numbered years, according to the Spring 1954 League of Women Voters booklet *The Hot Springs Story*, on file at the Garland County Historical Society.

## The System

The system includes political, social, and economic institutions that manifest into structural plans that have denied citizenship and humanity to black people since they were brought to this country. This book refers to three different meanings of the term "system."

The first meaning refers to the form of government known as mayor-alderman. In this meaning, a popularly elected mayor oversaw a council of aldermen. The aldermen each represented a district in the city known as a ward, even if they didn't live in the ward they represented. From 1921 until 1970, the city practiced this form of government with the condition that voters in an election could pick up to two aldermen from any ward, regardless of residency. It was virtually impossible for black candidates to win citywide as opposed to district-wide during that time.

The second meaning of the word "system" is the status quo that ensures white men will retain power in society. After the Emancipation Proclamation, many legalized tactics have attempted to keep blacks in a permanent underclass through Jim Crow, voter disenfranchisement, school segregation, high unemployment, mass incarceration, and the drug war waged mostly in black neighborhoods.

The third use of the word "system" is economic oppression. If wealth is inherited in this country from generation to generation, few black Americans have had little to pass down to their descendants. This stems from enslaved Africans toiling for 246 years receiving no payment and a broken promise of 40 acres and a mule.

While much wealth is obtained through homeownership, many black people were shut out of the American Dream through decades of legalized housing discrimination. Many lending institutions engaged in the practice of redlining, which denied loans to residents of who lived in primarily black or "urban" neighborhoods. And many black people were subjected to racially restrictive covenants—preventing them from living in certain neighborhoods—which were validated in 1926 by the U.S. Supreme Court in *Corrigan v. Buckley*. Also, after World War II, black soldiers returning home were denied access to government-funded housing developed specifically for veterans.

The system continues to stifle opportunities for black people. The salaries for many black employees were lower than white employees in Hot Springs during the Jim Crow era. Little has changed today. While a white woman makes 77 cents on a dollar to a white man, a black woman makes 64 cents on a dollar to a white man, according to the National Women's Law Center. In 2011, the median white household had $111,146 compared to $7,113 for the median black household, according to a March 2015 issue of *Forbes*.

As many black-owned businesses as there were in Hot Springs, black people faced many insurmountable obstacles when they attempted to open banks. The philanthropist John L. Webb was denied the chance to open a bank in the National Baptist Hotel and Bathhouse. In Greenwood, Oklahoma, black Americans managed to own banks, but angry white mobs destroyed them in the thriving black community known as Black Wall Street.

## Voting Rights

According to the U.S. Department of Justice, there were several federal laws prohibiting discrimination in election practices, but there was a stronger resistance to enforce voting rights by state officials. Then came the much applauded Voting Rights Acts of 1965 intended to ensure that all citizens would be allowed to exercise their constitutional right under the 15th Amendment. After facing months of immense pressure, President Lyndon B. Johnson signed the historic bill into law on August 6, 1965.

That was one year—almost to the day—after the bodies of murdered voting rights activists James Chaney, Michael Schwerner, and Andrew Goodman were found during Freedom Summer in Philadelphia, Mississippi. That also was six months—almost to the day—after peaceful protesters were assaulted by state troopers as they attempted to march across the Edmund Pettus Bridge on Bloody Sunday in Selma, Alabama.

This landmark civil rights legislation would put an end to disenfranchisement and discrimination in federal elections, but it did not put an end to the poll tax. The U.S. Supreme Court rejected many challenges to the Voting Rights Act in the four years following its passage, issuing this 1966 decision in *South Carolina v. Katzenbach*: "After enduring nearly a century of systematic resistance to the 15th Amendment, Congress might well decide to shift the advantage of time and inertia from the perpetrators of the evil to its victims."

In June 2013, *The New York Times* reported that the U.S. Supreme Court "struck down the heart of the Voting Rights Act of 1965." It referred to *Shelby County v. Holder* (2013). Now southern states are free to change their election laws without federal permission. The struggle continues.

## The Webb Community Center

John L. Webb, a developer and philanthropist, granted a building to the Negro community in 1945. He named it in honor of his daughter Emma Elease Webb. Today, it is more commonly known as the Webb Community Center and still operates at 127 Pleasant Street.

The center began as a two-story mansion. In later years, it became the present-day center of meeting rooms and a fellowship dining hall. It was once equipped with a basketball court and the only black public swimming pool. During segregation, the center provided a library for the black community, which was a rare find in those days.

Webb had applied for a license to open a bank in the National Baptist Hotel and Bathhouse in Hot Springs. The Arkansas Banking Commission rejected the application in

**Elmer Beard outside the Emma Elease Webb Center**

1926 for an unstated reason.

A book has been written about the life of Webb, titled *Triumph of the Simple Life of John L. Webb*, by Sutton E. Griggs. It was published in 1946 by the Messenger Publishing Company in Hot Springs.

### White Flight

White flight is the mass exit of white people from black or multi-racial areas. It became common, especially after the Great Migration of African Americans from the South to northern cities in the early to mid-20th Century. White flight isn't limited to south-to-north movement. When white people flee racially mixed areas, the exodus causes a negative ripple effect on tax bases, property values, school funding, and various quality of life issues.

# Support and Praise for
## *The Challengers*

This book is part of the NAACP Writing Project, a research committee of the NAACP Unit 6013 that documents local history in the African American community in Hot Springs National Park, Arkansas.

*The Challengers* was made possible in part by the generous contributions from Kenneth Rhodes, the Oaklawn Scholarship Foundation, the Arkansas Humanities Council, the Arkansas Black History Commission, and the Clinton Family Foundation.

======================

"I commend the NAACP Writing Project Committee for its extraordinary effort in preserving the history of African American involvement in the political process in the Spa City. This book demonstrates the courage of ordinary people who were determined to make a positive difference in the Hot Springs community. It is a treasure of information which I hope inspires greater participation in the political process by all people."
**Darrin L. Williams, CEO**

"This indispensable book tells the story of Hot Springs' African American community through its political aspirations from 1954–2010, a story that has never before been documented. Elmer Beard and the NAACP Writing Project Committee of NAACP Branch 6013 deserve the highest accolades for their exhaustive research and for their commitment to preserving the stories of the remarkable men and women in this book."
**Elizabeth Robbins**
**Executive Director, Garland County Historical Society**

"Elmer Beard's study of African American candidates for public office in Hot Springs and Garland County is a must read for students of local history and politics. With painstaking research he describes the political efforts of 63 African Americans who both won and lost contests over a period of more than a half century. On a personal note, the African American community gave me strong support in my elections for county judge, and I am happy to read about some of my friends in this book."
**Larry Williams**
**Garland County Judge 1995–2010**

"[This] provides an engaging look into the socio-political landscape of the City of Hot Springs, Arkansas, as it grapples with tense race relations before and after Jim Crow. At times humorous, other times tragic, but ultimately inspiring, this firsthand account underscores the importance of the continuing work of racial equality and social justice both locally and nationally."
**Minister Marsalis Weatherspoon**
**Hot Springs, Arkansas**

# About the Author

Elmer Beard is a poet, professor, and politician.

For the last 50 years, he has been a prominent leader in the African American community in Hot Springs National Park, Arkansas, where he and his late wife Dorothy reared their son and two daughters.

Beard has a bachelor's degree in English from Arkansas Baptist College in Little Rock and a master's degree in education from Henderson State University in Arkadelphia.

A self-appointed political griot of the Spa City, Beard has spent his career documenting the strides and struggles of black political candidates there. In *The Challengers*, Beard joins the local chapter of the NAACP to record profiles of the 63 black residents from 1954–2010 who dared to make a difference in their communities.

Now he issues a challenge for other NAACP chapters or civic organizations to record the black political history in their town in Arkansas and throughout the nation.